LEADING

LEADING BY EXAMPLE

Peter's Way for the Church Today

Graham Houston

Paternoster:
thinking faith

MILTON KEYNES ● COLORADO SPRINGS ● HYDERABAD

14 13 12 11 10 09 08   7 6 5 4 3 2 1

First published in 2008 by Paternoster
Paternoster is an imprint of Authentic Media
9 Holdom Avenue, Bletchley, Milton Keynes, Bucks, MK1 1QR, UK
1820 Jet Stream Drive , Colorado Springs, CO 80921, USA
OM Authentic Media, Medchal Road, Jeedimetla Village,
Secunderabad 500 055, A.P., India
www.authenticmedia.co.uk
Authentic Media is a division of IBS-STL U.K., limited by guarantee, with its
Registered Office at Kingstown Broadway, Carlisle, Cumbria CA3 0HA.
Registered in England & Wales No. 1216232. Registered charity 27016

British Library Cataloguing in Publication Data

A catalogue record for this book is available from
the British Library.

ISBN-13 978-1-84227-604-4

Design by James Kessell for Scratch the Sky Ltd (www.scratchthesky.com)
Print Management by Adare
Printed in Great Britain by J.H. Haynes and Co., Sparkford

Contents

Preface

This book is the product of nearly thirty-five years' experience in Christian leadership at various levels, as president of a student Christian Union, leader of parish mission and holiday mission teams, parish minister, ecumenical university chaplain and lecturer, and chief executive of a national Christian charity. During that time I have been involved in various publishing projects, including the publication of some of my poetry in a student newspaper, through serving as co-editor of a quarterly theological magazine, to editing a series of books on contemporary issues in Christian mission. In addition to a number of articles and book reviews I have authored three books which have addressed themes that have connected with my ongoing ministry and mission.

Many times during those years I have benefited from the teaching, counsel, and direction of Professor I. Howard Marshall, who instructed me in the scientific study of the Scriptures, and who is now Emeritus Professor of New Testament at the University of Aberdeen. Howard has been an invaluable guide during the process of writing this book, especially in keeping me up to date about relevant developments in New Testament studies. He also read closely the original manuscript and made many very helpful suggestions for improving the text. I must also acknowledge the considerable help and encouragement given during the writing of this book by Dr David Smith, Lecturer in Urban Mission and World Christianity at the International Christian College, Glasgow, who also provided insightful comments on the manuscript. My third recent source of academic scrutiny and guidance has been Professor John Swinton,

Professor of Practical Theology and Pastoral Care at the University of Aberdeen. To them I offer my sincere thanks.

Nearer to home my colleagues in the Church of Scotland's Presbytery of Lanark have challenged me to hone leadership skills and insights during the year they appointed me their Moderator, in 2006–7. I'm also grateful to my two congregations and their leaders in the beautiful South Lanarkshire rural parishes that we serve together, especially those who have dared to share in the ongoing process of learning by example. Above all, my wife Irene and our children Rachel, Rhoda (with husband Andy) and Stephen have been constant sources of support and encouragement, for which I am thankful to the Lord every day.

This volume is dedicated to the memory of the late Captain Stephen Anderson, Soldier, Shepherd, Evangelist and Mission Team Leader, who died ten years ago in 1998, from whom I learned much about leading by example.

Graham Houston
Manse of Cairngryffe with Symington
Easter 2008

Introduction

I expect that most of my readers remember where they were on 11 September 2001.

I heard on the radio of the first attack on the twin towers of the World Trade Center in New York. I switched on the television and saw the second impact live. The shock and horror of those scenes will live with me for the rest of my life. How on earth would the people of New York City cope with the first airborne assault against the mainland of the United States of America?

In the weeks and months that followed, it became clear that the city would work through the tragedy and would live again. In this process, one of the key factors was leadership. The then Mayor of New York City, Rudolph Giuliani, proved to be a man who could use the skills he had built up over many years of public service, including work as a US Public Attorney, for the benefit of all citizens. A practising Roman Catholic, yet a man who had come through a difficult divorce and remarriage and had been diagnosed with prostate cancer, Giuliani was nearing the end of his two four-year terms as Mayor. Other men might have taken this opportunity to take a back seat and let the President and the federal government take over. But Giuliani set about the task of motivating his fellow public servants and co-ordinating the various city services, such as the New York Police Department and the New York Fire Department, leading the city through the worst domestic disaster in US history.

In his best-selling book, *Leadership*,[1] Giuliani reflects on the principles which were in place in his management practices many years before 9/11, and which enabled him to handle a totally unforeseen disaster with complex human issues, because he had already assembled an excellent team and relied upon a systematic and methodical approach to decision-making and implementation. He counts leading to be a privilege, but also reckons with the heavy responsibilities that go with it, from developing a structure which is suited to the purposes of the organization, to gathering a team of people who work well together and challenge one another to take the appropriate risks.

The present book is written by a Christian leader with nearly thirty-five years of experience, mainly as parish minister, university chaplain/lecturer, and chief executive of a national charity. It is the third volume in the fields of Practical Theology and Christian Ethics, following *Prophecy Now* (1989) and *Virtual Morality* (1998). Transatlantic interchange has enriched my ministry and writing, and over the years I have been involved with exchange programmes and various cross-cultural projects involving Americans and Europeans. I respect and value those contacts, and enjoy friendship with a number of our ex-colonial cousins. Christian friends, a Baptist pastor from Maine and his wife, were with us for a meal in our home just a few days after 9/11, and I remember warmly the fellowship of suffering we shared that evening.

Yet, as my readers will discern in this book, these North American contacts have also made me question many aspects of our shared history, not least the ways in which Americans – as we British did in earlier days – have confidently sought to export all things American to the rest of the world.

As I have reviewed my own ministry a number of key texts authored in the US have helpfully influenced my theology and practice of ministry and mission. At the same time, however, there are other writings and programmes which have caused me to be concerned about the direction Protestant evangelicalism is taking in the early twenty-first century, in the cultural climate we have come to describe as postmodernity. In fact, what follows is the extension of the vision detailed in my first two books, now into the whole subject of church leadership.

My first book sought to encourage churches to recognize and release prophetic gifts in the contemporary church, and to escape from the stifling (and misconceived) ideas of some Reformed theologians, who have denied that prophecy is a continuing positive reality in the contemporary churches, to be viewed and used discerningly. My more recent contribution sought to show how classical Christian ethics is relevant in the complex world of computers and information technology. Again, my chief concern was that God's people might be further liberated to realize and experience the fuller dimensions of the Spirit's work in community life and effective mission, which God clearly wills for his worldwide church at this crucial time in human history. It is to that end that I offer this reflection on what leading meant for the apostle Peter and his associates, and to the churches which they sought to care for, and how that may be applied in the church and world of today and tomorrow.

Leading by Example completes a trilogy, and is intended as a resource for the churches which I hope will encourage leaders and those in leadership training, particularly in the mainstream traditional denominations, but also wherever true apostolic authority is recognized.

1

Lording It

I am on two boards. One is with a religious organization, and the other is with secular people. With the secular board members, I know that many are out for their own agenda. They manipulate and control and deceive. I know it, and so do they. But frankly, I've seen lots of the same controlling, manipulative, deceitful behaviour on the religious board. The difference is not the behaviour but in the fact that the secular board members often acknowledge their motives, whereas the believers don't. The believers not only deny them, but cover their motives with pious words. They talk spiritually, but they are playing the same game.[1]

In Shakespeare's *Hamlet* there is the famous one-liner about something being rotten in the state of Denmark. But the words quoted by Rebecca Pippert above are not from a work of drama or fiction. They were written by an international Christian businessman after many years of experience in various organizations, both religious and secular. The pain which they express is shared by many others who, like this anonymous servant of the Lord, have found that their involvement in Christian service has caused them not only heart-searching but also health problems, whether physical or mental or both. They have discovered, at personal cost, that there is something rotten in the state of the church in the twenty-first century.

Christian realists are not fazed by this conclusion. All human organizations, whether they have been established on Christian or on purely secular principles, are to be viewed realistically as both an opportunity and a threat to those who work in them and with them. Christians affirm the dignity of proper and honest organized work as an expression of human nature in God's image, yet recognize that every area of human experience is subject to the weaknesses caused by the fall of humankind into sin.

Domineering, then and now

Quoting the Greek poet and moralist Menander from his comedy *Thais*, the apostle Paul warned his churches that 'bad company corrupts good character' and related that to problems in the first century church of Corinth (1 Cor. 15:33). The problem for us as Christians today is that we may be largely unaware of the bad company we often keep with one another in churches and parachurch agencies. We are so often part of the problem rather than pointers to the solution, and our Christian character has often been impeached by double standards and dubious dealing. We may have found ourselves in congregations where the minister or priest is a bully or a demagogue, or where a coterie of elders, deacons or parish church council members constantly tries to control affairs with little concern to consult with or encourage other members of the body of Christ in that fellowship, all of whom have gifts they could exercise for the advancement of the Kingdom of God. We may know of so-called dynasty churches, even in rural areas, which have been dominated by certain families for generations. We may have experience of mission agencies which have treated their active servants as mere commodities that could be quietly disposed of when the board of directors felt they were no longer of use to the ministry; or we may know of senior executives of Christian charities who have effectively been removed and airbrushed out of the history of their organizations without the boards informing or consulting with the majority of their supporters.

So, what's new? In the first century CE[2] the apostle Peter had to deal with domineering Christian leaders when he was establishing churches in what we now call Turkey, and his treatment of 'lording it' is the focus of our Scripture search for material relevant to our theme:

> To the elders among you, I appeal as a fellow elder, and a witness of Christ's sufferings who also will share in the glory to be

revealed: Be shepherds of God's flock that is under your care, watching over them – not because you must, but because you are willing, as God wants you to be; not pursuing dishonest gain, but eager to serve; not lording it over those entrusted to you, but being examples to the flock. (1 Pet. 5:1–3)

The fact that Peter had to exhort church leaders not to lord it over their congregations shows that some were doing just that.

Around the time Peter was writing to churches throughout Asia Minor, north of the Taurus mountains, Paul was giving instructions to Titus, who had been left in charge of the work on the island of Crete, for the appointment of elders in every town. (As most readers probably know, elder (Gk. *presbyteros*) is the term used for those pastors who, in New Testament times, exercised the ministry of the word and prayer, either full-time and financially supported by the congregation, or as part-time tentmakers.)

> An **elder** must be blameless, faithful to his wife, a man whose children believe and are not open to the charge of being wild and disobedient. Since an **overseer** manages God's household, he must be blameless – not overbearing, not quick tempered, not given to drunkenness, not violent, not pursuing dishonest gain. Rather he must be hospitable, one who loves what is good, who is self-controlled, upright, holy and disciplined. He must hold firmly to the trustworthy message as it has been taught, so that he can encourage others by sound doctrine and refute those who oppose it (Tit. 1:6–9).

Thirty years later the aged apostle John, who, like Peter, described himself as 'the elder', would launch a broadside against one Diotrephes, about whom he warned a faithful elder called Gaius:

> I wrote to the church, but Diotrephes, who loves to be first, will have nothing to do with us. So if I come, I will call attention to what he is doing, spreading malicious nonsense about us. Not satisfied with that, he refuses to welcome other believers. He also stops those who want to do so and puts them out of the church. Dear friend, do not imitate what is evil but what is good (3 Jn. 9–11).

This church leader had set himself against the apostolic team and was defying apostolic authority. Instead of being hospitable to travelling missionaries, he was preventing them from being welcomed by the church near Ephesus in western Turkey. John denounced such behaviour as plain evil.[3]

Only one Lord

So lording it, being overbearing, and loving to be first are all aspects of this problem we might term empire-building, which is the very antithesis of true Christian leadership. Yet such behaviour is often condoned and excused today, despite our claims to be part of the one true catholic and apostolic church. The apostles directed that church leadership of this kind is an evil which must be dealt with and discouraged in all Christian congregations which want to be faithful to their Lord. Today, their guidance must also be applied to the increasing number of parachurch agencies and charities. Sadly, colleagues in leadership often do not have the courage to face this thorny issue of abuse by their fellows, with the result that many people may be estranged from congregations or Christian organizations because of the domineering attitudes and activities of a minority.

In this chapter we will focus on Peter's teaching and see how he addressed a problem which he considered to be very serious indeed. We will develop our discussion by allowing Peter, who once ran a family business in the Galilean fishing villages of Bethsaida and Capernaum, to engage in dialogue with the management-cultural factors typical of late modernity which have greatly influenced the shaping of twenty-first-century leadership styles in the churches, as exemplified in such popular works as Stephen Covey's *The 7 Habits of Highly Effective People*.[4]

As many readers may know, Covey's seven habits, or principles, which he believes to be self-evident, universal and timeless, are:

- Be proactive
- Begin with the end in mind
- Put first things first

- Think Win-Win
- Seek first to understand, then to be understood
- Synergize
- Sharpen the saw.

For Covey, being proactive is more than taking the initiative; it involves accepting responsibility for one's own behaviour (past, present, and future) and making decisions based on values and principles rather than on feelings or situations. We must begin, he asserts, by creating a mental vision and purpose for any project, which should result in the formulation of a mission statement. He believes that creating a culture behind a shared mission, vision, and values is the essence of leadership.[5] That is followed by focusing on what matters most as individuals and organizations. The main thing is to keep the main thing the main thing.[6] Win-Win thinking is not thinking selfishly or like a victim, but interdependently, in terms of We, not Me. It's sharing information, power, recognition, and rewards.[7] Effectiveness lies in getting the right balance between kindly seeking to understand and courageously seeking to be understood. This encourages a synergy, or creative co-operation, which is a third way in addition to yours or mine says Covey. Finally, the metaphor of saw-sharpening is about ongoing renewal in the four basic areas of life: physical, social/emotional, mental and spiritual.

Covey's approach achieved cult status in the 1990s, to such an extent that many echoes were produced for the Christian book scene, all of which gave some hope of success in ministry and mission through the careful adoption of management-culture styles of leadership in the churches and Christian agencies. Invariably, such seminal works on leadership have originated in North America and raise many issues about cross-cultural influences and the extent to which American authors are sufficiently aware of the cultural baggage which may be exported with their popular books. There is also the question of whether those who enthusiastically welcome their insights in the rest of the world are sensitive regarding their own vulnerability to an uncritical importation of inappropriate cultural styles and communication substance. In our discussion we will explore some of these global concerns with the help of intercultural expert Marvin K.

Mayers.[8] But where can we find immediate cross-cultural connections with Peter's teaching on church leadership? Is it not true that, over the centuries, Peter's role, and that of his alleged successors as overseers (bishops) of the Roman Catholic Church, have been very controversial and therefore problematic for developing modern models of ecclesiastical oversight?

The contemporary *Catechism of the Catholic Church*[9] claims a special place for Peter, asserting that 'When Christ instituted the Twelve, he constituted them in the form of a college or permanent assembly, at the head of which he placed Peter, chosen from among them; and so, in like fashion, Peter's successor, the Roman Pontiff,[10] and the successors of the apostles, the bishops, are related and united to one another.'[11] The *Catechism* goes on to claim that 'The Lord made Simon alone, whom he named Peter, the "rock" of his Church. He gave him the keys of his Church and instituted him shepherd of the whole flock.'[12] The logic of the apostolic succession is carried through rigorously in this important text: 'The Pope, Bishop of Rome and Peter's successor, is the perpetual and visible source and foundation of the unity both of the bishops and of the whole community of the faithful. For the Roman Pontiff, by reason of his office as Vicar of Christ, and as pastor of the entire Church has full, supreme, and universal power over the whole Church, a power which he can always exercise unhindered.'[13]

The *Catechism* goes on to outline the powers of bishops, who exercise pastoral care 'by ruling well their own churches as portions of the universal Church . . . The bishop is the steward of the grace of the supreme priesthood . . . the bishop and priests sanctify the Church by their prayer and work, by their ministry of word and sacraments . . . They sanctify her by their example, **not as domineering** over those in their charge, but as **examples** to the flock.'[14] The Church's history clearly reminds Catholics that such claims to absolute authority carry with them potential dangers. Even the title Pontiff is rooted not in the New Testament, but in the pre-Christian religion of Rome with its Pontifex Maximus, or High Priest of the state cultus.

How does this fit in with Peter's self-awareness as an apostle of Christ who had learned the hard way not to lord it over his people? To answer these and ancillary questions, we turn to

1 Peter, a letter claiming to be from the apostle. While some scholars assert that it cannot have been written by Peter himself, Howard Marshall and Earle Ellis have robustly argued that the traditional view, that Peter wrote the letter with the help of Silas and Mark, in Rome *c.* 63–64 CE, is preferable to claims for pseudonymity.[15] They show that arguments against Petrine authorship are unconvincing. The letter's good literary Greek style, for example, can be explained by the use of Silas (1 Pet. 5:12) as an amanuensis (secretary), yet we must not forget that a fisherman would have to be bilingual (Aramaic and Greek) in order to engage in business in cosmopolitan Galilee, as Carsten P. Thiede has shown.[16] In addition, they note that its authenticity was uncontested in the ancient church.

Why can we look with confidence to the practical theology of Simon Peter in this whole area of the priorities of cross-cultural Christian leadership? One key exemplar is found in the story of Peter's encounter with the Roman centurion, Cornelius, in Acts 10. 'Cornelius and his household ask Peter to stay with them for a few days; they need, and desire, further information.' Thiede makes this observation after reviewing the account: 'Peter's response casts a light on the priorities of an apostle and servant of Christ. Unlike the ecclesiastical leaders of today, the head of the young church is not ruled by his diary.'[17]

Peter at Rome

It has been argued that Peter went to Rome after his miraculous escape from prison in Jerusalem, as recorded in Acts 12. Thiede believes that Rome is the 'other place' which Luke mentions as Peter's destination (Acts 12:17), and that this is confirmed by the fourth-century historians Eusebius and Jerome, who say that Peter first set foot in Rome in 42 CE, during the second year of Claudius. Others, including Ellis, argue more convincingly that after his departure from Jerusalem, Peter probably based himself in Caesarea, where he had founded the first recorded Gentile church after the conversion of Cornelius and his household. Ellis holds this view mainly because of the extensive account provided by Luke in Acts concerning Peter's founding of the apostolic mission in that important port and Roman military base (Acts 10:1–48; 11:1–18; 15:7–11). Peter's encounter with Cornelius, and the connected vision, led to a remarkable lifestyle change for Peter, including a break with Jewish food laws, even though it was fitful at times. Ellis argues that this explains Peter's presence at nearby Jerusalem for Paul's famine visit in 46 CE (Gal. 2:10) and at the Council of Jerusalem in 50 CE, where he played second fiddle to James (Acts 15:4–29), and also accounts for Peter's mission in Syrian Antioch in 49 ce.[18] Peter may have travelled via Antioch and several towns in Asia Minor (probably including some in those regions addressed in 1 Peter) and Corinth (1 Cor. 1:12,14; 9:5), and then to Rome, arriving in 53 or 54 CE, during Claudius's reign, as attested in the second century by Irenaeus.

In view of this analysis we have to question whether Peter should be recognized historically as the first apostle to establish the church officially in Rome, as Thiede proposes. After all, Paul later stated that in his planned visit to the Roman Christians he did not want to build on another's foundation.[19] Before the Claudian expulsions of 49 CE there were 50,000 Jews in Rome, with whom Peter would doubtless have began his mission had he gone there at a much earlier date, probably building on the witness of those recorded in Acts 2:10 as visitors from Rome in Jerusalem at Pentecost. Even if we were to accept the view that Peter arrived in Rome in 42 CE, he was probably away from Rome from 44 to 46 ce, engaging in ecumenical business leading up to the Council of Jerusalem (Acts 15:1ff), which could explain the text's silence about Peter's activities between Acts 12:17 and 15:7. In Galatians 2:11 ff, Paul speaks of Peter's visit to Antioch,[20] when they disagreed about policy regarding their ministry among Jewish Christians, about which Thiede comments on 'Peter's display of flexible leadership', and that 'Peter's style of leadership had proved acceptable to the Christians in Antioch.' Interestingly, Peter is the only New Testament writer, apart from Luke (Acts 11:26; 26:28) who refers to believers as Christians (1 Pet. 4:16). Luke says that it was in Antioch that the title was first applied to the growing church (Acts 11:26).

Peter's pattern

Peter, apostle of Jesus Christ (1 Pet. 1:1), later wrote his first letter to a number of churches with which he apparently had connections (but which are not mentioned in Acts) in the Roman provinces of Asia (which became part of the Empire in 133 BCE), Bithynia and Pontus (63 BCE), Galatia (25 BCE),[21] and Cappadocia (17 CE) and which together covered the lion's share of Asia Minor, a region of the ancient world that corresponds roughly to modern-day Turkey. Jewish adherents from those regions had been in Jerusalem on the Day of Pentecost (Acts 2:9–11), and Paul had preached and taught in some of these provinces. Peter numbered the believers there among God's chosen people who had been dispersed according to the Lord's purposes and plans. They had been set apart by the Spirit for obedience to Jesus Christ (Acts 1:2), so he reminded them. But they were probably mostly of Gentile background, some very new to the faith (2:2), as he speaks of their former ignorance of the living God (1:14), spiritual darkness (2:9), and pagan vices (4:3–4), although there were undoubtedly Jewish Christians too, as there are many quotations from the Greek translation of the Old Testament. 1 Peter reflects the history and terminology of the Gospels and Acts, and in particular echoes Luke's record of Peter's speeches (in Acts 2–5; 11–12), and it resonates, both thematically and conceptually, with Peter's experiences and associations during the three-year ministry of Jesus of Nazareth.[22] The early churches accepted the Petrine authorship of this letter, and Clement, who may have succeeded Peter as bishop of Rome, indicates his acquaintance with 1 Peter in his own first letter (*c.* 70 CE). Again, Polycarp, bishop of Smyrna in the province of Asia, the martyr and disciple of the apostle John, clearly made use of 1 Peter in his letter to the Philippian church early in the second century.

As a Galilean fisherman, Peter would have had Aramaic as his mother tongue, but he would also have learned to use *koinē* (common) Greek, which was the language of commerce in the eastern Mediterranean at the time, and the dialect used by the New Testament writers. The letter reflects the turmoil which was typical of the situation for Christians during the reign of the Emperor Nero (54–68 CE), and some scholars suggest that it may have been

written in the early 60s, probably from Rome, code-named
Babylon (5:13). 1 Peter shows familiarity with letters which Paul
wrote during his Roman house arrest around that time:
Philippians, Ephesians and Colossians. (For example, compare
1:1–3 with Ephesians 1:1–3; 2:18 with Colossians 3:22; and 3:1–6
with Ephesians 5:22–24.) Peter himself was martyred, according to
early Christian tradition, in Rome, towards the end of Nero's reign.
Before his demise, it is very likely that he would urgently have
exhorted the churches with a series of ethical imperatives, a feature
which runs through the letter from 1:13 to 5:11. Here is a selection:

> With minds that are alert and fully sober . . . do not conform to the
> evil desires you had when you lived in ignorance . . . Be holy . . .
> Live out your time as foreigners here . . . Love one another deeply,
> from the heart . . . Rid yourselves of all malice and all deceit,
> hypocrisy, envy and slander . . . Crave pure spiritual milk . . .
> Abstain from sinful desires . . . Live such good lives among the
> pagans that (. . .) they may see your good deeds and glorify God
> . . . Submit yourselves for the Lord's sake, to every human author-
> ity: whether to the emperor, as the supreme authority, or to gover-
> nors . . . Live as free people, but do not use your freedom as a
> cover-up for evil . . . Live as God's slaves . . . Show proper respect
> to everyone . . . Love your fellow believers, fear God, honour the
> emperor . . . Be like-minded . . . Be sympathetic, love one another,
> be compassionate, and humble. Do not repay evil with evil, or
> insult with insult. On the contrary repay evil with blessing . . . Be
> alert and of sober mind . . . Offer hospitality to one another with-
> out grumbling . . . Each one should use whatever gift you have
> received to serve others, as faithful stewards of God's grace in its
> various forms. If you speak, you should do so as one who speaks
> the very words of God. If you serve, you should do so with the
> strength God provides . . . Rejoice in as much as you participate in
> the sufferings of Christ . . . Those who suffer according to God's
> will should commit themselves to their faithful Creator and con-
> tinue to do good . . . Greet one another with a kiss of love.

So Peter was passionate about the very issues which we are
addressing in this book, and is well qualified to be our organizational advisor in the twenty-first century, just as he was for those

early Christians in the first. Like Jesus the Joiner, Peter the Fisherman knew what it was like to manage a family business,[23] and could not separate his work ethic from personal, familial, or spiritual morality. He did not have double standards,[24] in other words, and did not imagine that Christian service or family values could be exercised according to one set of ethical constraints, while daily duties, both civil and occupational, were placed in another box. It was a matter of being faithful to the Way, as followers of the Christian way of life (cf. Acts 9:2; 24:14). That is why he uses the word 'live' several times in the above compendium of exhortations – Christians are to live as pilgrims travelling through foreign territory, yet living outstanding lives, so that the natives give God the glory rather than drawing attention to themselves. They are to live in freedom without taking liberties, yet be willing servants of their Lord. They should live in such harmony with one another that their attitudes clearly reflect the character and commitment of Christ himself.

In this way, Peter exhorts his hearers, 'Submit, for the Lord's sake, to every human authority' (in the secular world, 2:13ff), and 'Submit yourselves to your elders' (in the church, 5:5ff). His instructions to church leaders must, therefore, be understood in context, if valid connections are to be made with parallel problems that we may face in the contemporary world and church. If we are right in suggesting that authoritarianism and empire-building are very serious problems in today's church, we have to ask whether there is any theological or ethical justification for such leadership styles in the teaching of the apostles themselves.[25] We are also aware that the Islamic world claims to be faithful in submission to God (Allah) through their prophet, Muhammad, as the word Muslim in Arabic means 'one who submits'. So we have to understand the difference, in Peter's mind, between the proper exercising of ecclesiastical authority and what he describes as 'lording it'.[26] But let's remember at the outset what is at stake in this debate. It is not about semantics, but concerns our convictions about who has the right of Lordship over all our lives, and how that authority is to be exercised. The first Christians proclaimed that Jesus Christ is Lord, but never accepted coercion[27] as an appropriate way to bring people under his gracious rule. They preached the message of his Lordship and

planted congregations in the Roman Empire, the emissaries of
which, in contrast, asserted the ultimate sovereignty of Caesar,
and established and maintained his reign by force. Most of my
readers will live in countries which enjoy a considerable measure
of political and individual freedom. Yet many contemporary
Christians imagine that domination is appropriate behaviour, in
the church, for those who profess faith in Christ as Lord and say
that they are doing his business.

However, we all have a choice, as we enter into discussion
about this important set of issues. We don't need to accept the
unreasonable rule of those who try to dominate others, and this
book aims to provide a way forward, not only for those who have
been victims of domineering church leadership, but also for those
who have found themselves drawn into behaving that way themselves as leaders, and long to be free. This book is dedicated to all
earnest and realistic Christians who pray that all the churches
may grow up into Christ, the Image of God who holds all things
together (Col. 1:15–17). At the end of the day, as Bob Dylan so
aptly observed in his 1979 album *Slow Train Coming*, 'It may be the
devil, or it may be the Lord, but you're gonna have to serve somebody . . .' Whether we like it or not, somebody has to be in ultimate charge of our lives, and the dynamics of leading and being
led are parts of everyday experience. Let's explore together what
leading by example, Peter's way, is really all about. Join me on a
journey down one road which we all need to travel, before it's too
late.

Summary

Let's summarize where we've been in this opening chapter:

- We've faced the fact that many contemporary Christians, both
  those in leadership positions and those who are glad just to be
  followers of Jesus, have been subjected to domineering attitudes and actions by bona fide church leaders.
- We've recognized that this is no new phenomenon, but that it
  was present in the church as early as the first century of the
  Christian era, and dealt with by the apostles. In those days,

empire-building was a way of life for the Romans, and many of the first disciples were living in territories under military occupation and governance. But there could be only one Lord, Jesus Christ, who could expect the ultimate loyalty and obedience of believers.

- We've noted that the apostle Peter, in particular, was concerned about this issue, for very good reasons. Not only did he have the responsibility of establishing cross-cultural leadership styles and patterns in the congregations with which he was connected; he had formerly been in business and understood the temptations which Christian leaders faced to transfer worldly management methodology to their exercising of authority in the church.

2

Strange Stories – Peter's and Ours

One very good reason for focusing on Peter's teaching about leadership is that we can often identify with him more readily than with his contemporary, Paul of Tarsus. The New Testament is not short of criticism of the fisherman, and even the Gospel of Mark, which we believe to have been informed by the author's close relationship with Peter, pulls no punches in putting Peter in his place! Along with his travelling companion Luke, Paul was, of course, the most prolific writer in the apostolic communities, so we often see the early church from a Pauline perspective. We know much more about his missionary methods than Peter's, simply because of the thirteen letters we have which deal with the most significant issues faced by the earliest Christian churches. But we must not forget the fact that Peter is presented by Luke as the chief character of the first twelve chapters of Acts, where he has to grapple with some of the key leadership issues which arose in those early days. They may read like strange stories to us, but let me assure you that the worldwide church of Christ today is not short of peculiarities. In this book we will set out to put our readings of Peter's teaching in the contexts we find ourselves in today within the Catholic and evangelical traditions, which together make up the vast majority of professing Christians in today's world. Since the Second Vatican Council in the 1960s the former have struggled to reassess the proper place of Peter as 'Prince of the Apostles', and indeed the way the Roman Catholic Church relates to non-Catholics through its hierarchy. The latter have often awarded de facto supremacy to Paul, following the lead of Martin Luther and other reformers of the sixteenth century, at least in theological terms. However, while most evangelicals claim to follow Paul's doctrinal emphases, few are aware of the significance of Peter's *paraenesis* (ethical exhortation),[1] and most are bemused and annoyed by Roman Catholic insistence on continued deference to Peter as the first pope of Rome and by continued claims to Roman supremacy over the universal church. Yet conservative Christians of all persuasions find themselves in a postmodern climate which questions all authority claims and often consigns committed Christianity to the realm of fantasy.

Peter's example

Despite this questioning, our theme implies that it is possible to derive appropriate ways of being and doing from the example of others. Peter urges Christian leaders to exercise leadership without domineering but rather by making a positive impression: '. . . not lording it over those entrusted to you, but being examples to the flock' (1 Pet. 5:3). The Greek word for example found here is *typos*, the root of the English word type. We use that word for classification, but it is also the word adopted for the metal characters which printers traditionally used for their craft. In earlier times the manuscript of this book would have been written on a typewriter, and one could observe the impression made on the paper by its function in the machine. There is something of that idea in the original language. Peter is speaking of leading as making an impression on others, or of leaving a mark.[2] That is not to say that domineering leaders do not impress others. It is rather that they do so in an overbearing way, and make the wrong kind of impression. They are too heavy-handed and authoritarian, says Peter. The problem is that, for some people, such leadership styles are attractive, probably because those who are led are willing to sacrifice their critical abilities to a considerable extent and more or less unquestioningly accept the domination of their leaders.

Peter's warning here echoes the teaching of Mark 10:42–45: 'You know that those who are regarded as rulers of the Gentiles lord it over them, and their high officials exercise authority over them. Not so with you. Instead, whoever wants to become great among you must be your servant, and whoever wants to be first must be slave of all. For even the Son of Man did not come to be served but to serve, and to give his life as a ransom for many.' In contrast to lording it over others, Peter promotes the imitation of God in Christ as the only valid approach to leading by example. 'Just as he who called you is holy, so be holy in all you do; for it is written, "Be holy, because I am holy"' (1 Pet. 1:15–16, quoting Lev. 11:44. Cf. Mt. 5:48, 'Be perfect as your heavenly Father is perfect'; Lk. 6:36, 'Be merciful just as your Father is merciful.') Again, Peter stresses his main point: 'How is it to your credit if you receive a beating for doing wrong and endure it? But if you suffer for doing good and you endure it, this is commendable before God. To this you were called, because Christ suffered for you, leaving you an example, that you should follow in his steps' (1 Pet. 2:20–23). Here the Greek word *hypogrammos* involves the idea of setting a pattern of behaviour.

What is interesting as we explore Christian patterns of leading connected with Peter is that his discussion in 1 Peter is clearly related to the stories in which he features in Mark's Gospel.[3] It is there that we find the example of which he speaks in his letter, and which he urges his hearers to follow. Some of the narratives do not paint a very positive picture of Peter's attitudes or actions. So we need to take some time to look at those strange stories and determine how it is that they became exemplars for Christian leaders, and may continue to be so today.

The type of leader who impressed Peter was, of course, exemplified in Jesus himself.[4] The gospel narrative in Mark soon focuses on the encounter of Jesus with four fishermen. It doesn't say that this was their first meeting, and John 1:35–42 suggests that there was an earlier encounter. Mark is keen to show us that, from the beginning, Jesus made an impression by his intriguing sayings. He catches Peter's attention, and then says he is going to teach him, and the others, how to do a similar kind of thing to what they were doing in their daily work, but with a difference. As the men went about their business, catching fish with a net, Jesus calls out to them, 'Come, follow me, and I will send you out to fish for people' (Mk. 1:17). This seems to be loaded with humour and uses the first powerful metaphor which Jesus, as spiritual master, adopted. As the archetypal leader, Jesus invites his followers to come and learn to catch in a new way. There will be connections with their experience up to that point, but he has plans to lead them into new territory. From the beginning, Christian leadership is to be focused on teaching, but teaching which is rooted in experience and relationships, and with practical outcomes.

Peter's *paraenesis*

We see here the emphasis which Peter later expounded in his first letter, which we have called his paraenetic approach. Later in that chapter Mark tells us about the healing of Peter's mother-in-law, and the healing ministry of Jesus which ensued (Mk. 1:29–34), followed by Jesus' early morning prayer time outside Capernaum to get away from the crowds. Peter and the others seek him out and Jesus emphasizes that he has to move on from there to other places. He has to preach, because that is why he came (1:35–39). Preaching and healing/exorcism always go together in Mark, because all are good news of God's Kingdom. So it is no surprise that when Jesus eventually chooses twelve key people to join with him in his mission and ministry, they are to be with him, to be sent out to preach, and to drive out demons.

Simon Peter is named first on the list, explaining the origin of his nickname, Rock (3:16). In 5:37, relating the story of the healing of Jairus' daughter, Mark tells us that only Peter, James and John were allowed to go with Jesus to Jairus' house. Yet later on, when Peter declares that he believes Jesus to be the Messiah (8:27–30), Mark does not include Christ's statement 'on this rock I will build my church', which is found in Matthew 16:13–20. Peter's position is not important to Mark here, and there is no claim to any unique role. Again, in the next chapter, Mark tells the story of the Transfiguration, where Peter, James and John are taken up a mountain by Jesus for a strange encounter with long-dead Moses and Elijah. We are not spared the embarrassment of Peter's inept reaction, 'Rabbi, it is good for us to be here! Let us put up three shelters . . . (He did not know what to say, they were so frightened)' (Mk. 9:5–6). Later, Peter was careful to note that this encounter with great heroes of faith was no mythical scene: 'We did not follow cleverly devised stories when we told you about the coming of our Lord Jesus Christ in power, but we were eyewitnesses of his majesty' (2 Pet. 1:16). The telling referred to may well mean the story as recorded by Mark. The Greek word for eyewitness literally means 'spectator'.[5] Peter claims that he really was there when this unique event happened. The only other time we read of Peter speaking up before the Passion narrative is after the story of the rich young man whose love of wealth prevented him from following Jesus, in Mark 10:28: 'We have left everything to follow you!' After the Last Supper Jesus predicted his imminent death and the scattering of his disciples, to which Peter retorted, 'Even if all fall away, I will not' (14:29). When Jesus then made his statement about Peter's denying him three times, Peter replied, 'Even if I have to die with you, I will never disown you', but, of course, he couldn't even stay awake in the garden, let alone stay with Jesus through his ordeal. His denial of Jesus was very public, in the courtyard of the High Priest's house. Rather than remaining loyal to Jesus, he broke down and cried. He then vanishes from the scene, with no further explanation. The only other mention of Peter in Mark is in the angelic message to the women at the resurrection: 'But go, tell his disciples and Peter' (16:7). Despite his denial, Peter is, after all, to be included in what is about to unfold.

It is that sense of being graciously dealt with by Christ,[6] despite all Peter's many human weaknesses and foibles, that pervades Mark's account. Whatever Christian leadership is to be like in the apostolic communities, and in the expanding churches which they planted, it is not rooted in triumphalism. There is no attempt to portray Peter and his friends as larger than life heroes in the Hellenistic traditions which they would have well known and understood. The Hebraic prophets such as Moses and Elijah also paled into insignificance when compared with Jesus the Christ. It is a form of leadership which relies on the inspired message revealed through the historical events of Christ's life, death and resurrection, of which Peter and the others were participants and not merely observers. To follow Jesus into Christian leadership meant becoming good news people, not merely those who shared their testimony of the mighty acts of God in history of which they were eyewitnesses, but those whose lives demonstrated the realities of which they preached. From the beginning, leading the church would, by definition, mean a living out of the truths believed and proclaimed. Authentic Christian leadership would be leading by example. This theme was later taken up by Shakespeare: 'Do not, as some ungracious pastors do, show me the steep and thorny way to heaven, whiles, like a puff'd and reckless libertine, himself the primrose path of dalliance treads, and recks[7] not his own advice' (*Hamlet*).

This book asks some very big questions of the models which some contemporary Christian leaders have chosen to adopt. In particular, we will be addressing the extent to which trends in leadership style and substance are rooted in coherent contemporary theologies of mission and ministry, and whether they are sensitive to and conversant with the range of culture-formative influences which are typically postmodern.

If we look back over the last twenty-five years or so we can trace the influence of certain movements which have provided motivation for leadership within evangelical churches in the West. The 1970s were marked by the body-life teaching of Ray Stedman[8] from California. At that time, Restorationist ecclesiology was also being developed by the house church movement in Britain.[9] The 1980s were years of ascendancy for charismatic emphases, exemplified by the ministry of the late John Wimber,[10] also from California, with his Vineyard group of churches, although the late David Watson,[11] an Anglican from York in England, shared some of his emphases and had greater impact for many evangelical leaders in Britain, especially those who chose to remain within the traditional denominations. The 1990s saw the rise of the Willow Creek churches modelled on the Chicago experience of Bill Hybels and the 'seeker-friendly' megachurch.[12] The new millennium was heralded with yet another set of ideals as promoted by Rick Warren's Purpose Driven Church[13] approach, from California. The most recent movement in this series of exports from North America has been the so-called Emerging Church.[14] For those of us in Europe who are concerned about the uncritical importation of culturally charged church influences from North America, this brief resume should suffice to provide sources for the strange stories which characterize the search for appropriate and effective leadership in twenty-first-century churches. Let me share some which enable us to contextualize our discussion.

Six stories

Malcolm[15] served overseas as a mission partner, then returned to be the pastor of an evangelical church in his homeland, during which time he also got very involved in the work of a parachurch agency. Eventually he was elected chairman of its board, and then was invited to become its full-time CEO, so that he left the ministry for management, despite having had no hands-on experience in that field. Over a considerable period of time Malcolm worked very hard to develop the organization's outreach and increase its charitable income, with much success. He got involved in the international fellowship to which his organization was affiliated, and was earmarked for positions of influence in the committee structures. However, while he was cultivating a wider international role, behind the scenes some of his senior colleagues were complaining that he was out of the country far too much, and that they were being left to carry the can. When he did spend time in his office, they said that they often felt bullied and cajoled into doing his bidding, rather than being consulted and involved in the process of major decision-making. Some of those who worked with him sensed that he had still higher aspirations. Their hunches proved right when he was approached to become CEO of the international agency and accepted the post, but his departure left a bitter taste in the mouths of some of his former subordinates, who felt that he had used them to gain further power and position. And yet, at home and abroad, he had made quite a name for himself, as an effective manager and visionary conference speaker. He had sought new leadership resources to inform and inspire, driven by a desire to be more effective and to influence others, and confessed that he had become very influenced by the books of management guru Stephen Covey. We will return to this theme in chapter 9, where we will ask whether Covey's insights and assertions are really resonant with biblical leadership as exemplified in Peter's paraenesis.

Grace grew up as a pastor's daughter and from early days felt called to missions. After her college and theological education she committed herself to the establishing of a new kind of outreach based in Europe, which was consciously set up to try to avoid some of the cultural imperialism to which we have already alluded. She set about living with the people, learning their language and building community. Through her a number of young people committed their lives to Christ and volunteers were happy to join her from her homeland to help in the growing work. Some of the nationals who had come to Christ responded to a call to full-time Christian service in various church ministries, and the influence grew in one particular denomination. Links were established with sister churches in other countries, and creative exchanges were organized which enabled young people to serve both in Europe and in the US. Concerns were expressed on a number of occasions that groups coming from the States tended to bring with them preconceived agendas and a conviction that their way of doing things was non-negotiable. But any such questioning was dismissed without proper discussion. Then, some years into the work, a number of those who were involved began to be concerned about Grace's need to control the situations over which she had leadership, and were worried that she was suffering from stress and making poor judgments about the involvement of some of the young people. However, she and the organizing group stateside shrugged off any suggestions that things were going pear-shaped. It was several years before they accepted that there was anything major wrong with the operation, despite the early intervention of one respected European Christian leader. His warnings had simply been ignored. The situation became serious when Grace had a breakdown and complaints were levelled by parents of young people with whom she was working. She was called home and asked to undergo counselling. But soon the agenda of her group leaders was made known. They were not prepared to let her return to Europe under their aegis, and they were withdrawing their support. It was as if her years of service, during which she had built up a network of Christian contacts in a number of countries, were being rubbished. Yet Grace, after a time of reflection and treatment, continued to believe that God was calling her in mission, and returned to Europe with the blessing of some close friends, but without the support of those who had for many years been her mission base. The sea change which had occurred seemed inexplicable.

George was brought up in a working-class environment and worked hard to enable him to rise above his relatively poor origins, eventually training as a solicitor. He later felt called into the ministry of the church and served for a time in a rural parish, before taking up an appointment in the central administration of his denomination, a department with hundreds of employees across the nation. He got a reputation for no-nonsense, hard-nosed management, and gained a number of admirers. However, many who worked under him saw another side to his purposeful, proud, and enthusiastic leadership style. In fact, one lady felt so aggrieved that she very nearly took him to an employment tribunal, and others complained of his bombastic methods which often left participants in meetings feeling belittled and deskilled. When he retired, he continued to be involved in a major Christian agency in a leadership position, and often bullied his way through meetings, which he adjudged to be successful if they were completed within his projected time span without any objections being raised to the policies that he was pushing through! He often failed to listen to key officers of the organization when they complained about increased workload, brushing off their hesitations with what he thought were compliments about their abilities to cope. In reality, he seemed to be oblivious to the real needs and aspirations of many of the people with whom he worked. Selfism ruled his life, although he would have been very offended if such an allegation had been made. Most of his associates, if truth be told, were too scared of him to tell him the truth!

Stanley was brought up in a keen Christian home, and his father was a lay preacher. He left school and soon developed his own business, which was very successful. He got very involved in his local church, which grew and made a real impact in the community. Then there came the need to move to a bigger building, and Stanley was able to provide a considerable amount of the capital needed to engage in a large-scale building project. The problem was that the new church was so associated with Stanley and his family that the leaders kowtowed to them and they increasingly believed that they should have the lion's share of influence over the direction taken by the congregation. It was as if they were controlling a company of which they had the largest shareholding. This alienated a number of members and eventually led to Stanley's leaving the church and moving away from the community.

Patrick served in the armed forces and then trained for pastoral ministry, developing an emphasis on expository preaching and corporate prayer. His church became a focus for Christian work among students, and Patrick's preaching was greatly appreciated. But some of those who shared in church leadership with him became very uneasy with his authoritarian style and his apparent inability to delegate. One of the leaders was a very keen supporter of mission organizations, for which the church regularly prayed, and so he suggested at a meeting that the congregation should produce a booklet containing the details of each missionary family. He himself would have been very able and willing to do the work required, but Patrick seemed to take his suggestion as a personal criticism and dismissed it with the statement, 'I don't have time to do that.' End of story! In contrast with some of the other leaders in the congregation, another leader, Maurice, who had been greatly influenced by Patrick since student days, did indeed seem to submit blindly to him with sycophantic zeal. And when his mentor retired, it was alleged that Maurice was attempting to ensure, behind the scenes, that the church called a man after his own heart as a successor to his hero. In fact, it proved to be the case that he was prepared to use people as means to ends in order to attain whatever goals he cherished. As psychiatrist Paul Vitz notes, 'When human beings are treated more and more objectively, various problems arise. The development of objective knowledge intrinsically involves a power relationship: the subject (self) has power over the object.'[16] This is the kind of organizational behaviour which Maurice learned from Patrick, albeit unwittingly, and it is not unusual in Reformed and evangelical churches. In fact, it reflects the modern Western culture in which we lived through the twentieth century, rather than radically reflecting real Christian leadership. 'This culture is marked by . . . reducing all relations to the question: "What am I getting out of it?"'[17] Maurice, like many of his contemporaries, was simply caught up with what Vitz calls 'society's fascination with self-aggrandizement'. Vitz continues, 'Life has become a game where there are only two states, winning and losing.' Maurice had come to see his religious commitment as a struggle for supremacy and power over others, rather than as selfless service. He began to exploit the vulnerability of others, turning their sharing of personal needs into opportunities to exercise control over them, even daring to dissuade younger members of the congregation from getting engaged if Maurice and his wife did not approve! But what he did not realize was that he was on a very slippery slope; as Vitz says, 'If you show weakness, i.e. a need for love, you get slaughtered; if you withdraw to a machine-like, emotion-free competence and develop complete identification with career, you are isolated and starved for intimacy and love.'[18]

Self-evident or scriptural?

This book is written with compassion for people like Maurice, Patrick, Stanley, George, Grace, and Malcolm, who have – I hope inadvertently – misshaped their own lives, and the lives of many of those they have sought to control, through distorted patterns of leadership. That is something which Simon Peter understood very well, on and after the Day of Pentecost. For in his speech to the crowd on that momentous day, he not only invited his hearers to repent and be baptized, but called them to 'Save yourselves from this corrupt generation' (Acts 2:40). This echoes the Old Testament phrase for the people of Israel who rebelled against God in the desert: 'They are corrupt and not his children; to their shame they are a warped and crooked generation' (Deut. 32:5). It also connects with some of the sayings of Jesus in Luke, as when his disciples were not able to drive out a demon: 'You unbelieving and perverse generation, how long will I stay with you and put up with you?' (Lk. 9:41). Again, when crowds followed Jesus, only looking for miracles, he angrily responded, 'This is a wicked generation. It asks for a sign, but none will be given it except the sign of Jonah . . . The people of Nineveh will stand up at the judgment with this generation and condemn it; for they repented at the preaching of Jonah, and now one greater than Jonah is here' (Lk. 11:29, 32). In the New Testament letters, the same assessment is made of those who are under pressure to reject Jesus: 'Do everything without grumbling or arguing, so that you may become blameless and pure, "children of God without fault in a warped and crooked generation"' (Phil. 2:14–15), and 'That is why I was angry with that generation; I said, "Their hearts are always going astray, and they have not known my ways"' (Heb. 3:10). Yet, lest we become complacent, imagining that we could never relapse into generational sin – patterns of corporate thought and behaviour which militate against God's kingdom – the writer to the Hebrews goes on to say, 'See to it, brothers and sisters, that none of you has a sinful, unbelieving heart that turns away from the living God. But encourage one another daily . . . so that none of you may be hardened by sin's deceitfulness. We have come to share in Christ if we hold firmly till the end our original conviction' (Heb. 3:12–14).

We see from this how Peter's realistic Christian worldview underlies his expanding apostolic ministry from the Day of Pentecost until his martyrdom in Rome, some thirty-five years later. It stems from his own brokenness as described by Mark and Luke. He saw himself as one of that corrupt generation which is constantly tempted to deny the Lord, as Peter did before his restoration. That's why his letters contain references to the need for growth and perseverance in the Christian life:

> Praise be to the God and Father of our Lord Jesus Christ! In his great mercy he has given us new birth into a living hope through the resurrection of Jesus Christ from the dead, and into an inheritance that can never perish, spoil, or fade. This inheritance is kept in heaven for you, who through faith are shielded by God's power until the coming of the salvation that is ready to be revealed in the last time. In all this you greatly rejoice, though now for a little while you may have had to suffer grief in all kinds of trials. These have come so that your faith – of greater worth than gold, which perishes even though refined by fire – may be proved genuine and may result in praise, glory and honour when Jesus Christ is revealed (1 Pet. 1:3–7).

> For this very reason, make every effort to add to your faith goodness; and to goodness knowledge; and to knowledge self-control; and to self-control perseverance (2 Pet. 1:5–6).

One of the great weaknesses of contemporary Western Christian leaders is lack of insight into the influence of indwelling sin and personal evil,[19] in their own lives as well as in those of their flocks, and a tendency towards various shades of triumphalism.[20] A number imagine that the pattern of their own ministry is of universal application, to be exported uncritically to other situations. Some even proclaim the relevance and applicability of their insights to be 'self-evident'. That's the essence of spiritual empire-building, or lording it. Peter's strange stories, and ours, are intended to enable leaders who have discovered that they are not the ideal models for the church which they once proudly imagined themselves to be, to refocus and realize that the only examples we need are found in the word of God, the scriptures of Old and New Testaments, as fulfilled in the Word made flesh, Jesus Christ. The rest of this book will seek to unpack the implications of this insight, with the help of the apostle Peter and contemporary Christian thinkers and leaders.

Summary

Let's summarize the main points of this chapter:

- Peter's experience was an example both of what to do and of what not to do.
- Peter's paraenesis is based on his own personal need for ethical exhortation.
- Contemporary experts often attract adherents because of claims to self-evident insights and effectiveness, while Jesus and the apostles persuaded their hearers by the application of scriptural principles.
- Peter's strange stories should be contrasted with contemporary claims to success in management and ministry.

3

Rhetoric and Resident Aliens

Let's think a bit more about what Peter was attempting to achieve through his first circular letter to the scattered Christian congregations in Asia Minor. New Testament scholars term his approach *paraenesis*, which means 'ethical exhortation', and which is paralleled in Hellenistic (Greek-speaking) culture in the first century CE. Peter was using a well-tried and widely understood way of attempting to motivate his hearers, in other words. As we noted in chapter 1, he reminded them that they had begun a new way of life in Christ. They had received the teaching of Jesus and his apostles, and had committed themselves to a lifestyle which involved carrying out the instructions which they had received when first they had professed faith and were baptized into the Christian community. Peter was taking this further by underlining other ethical principles and rules which are typical of the Christian way of life when it is lived to the full, so that a lasting impact is made on the, as yet, unbelieving world around. In this way, Peter was outlining those features of Christian conviction and commitment which are essential for Christian identity.[1]

In other words, faithfully following Jesus makes a real and positive difference to the everyday living of ordinary Christian people, without drawing attention to self, and influences their neighbours for good and for God. That is as much a part of the good news as the great central truths of the Christian proclamation, such as the sacrifice of Christ for sinners. In fact, those who preach the gospel can be truly effective only when their message is embodied in the Christian community.[2] Christianity is based on the fact of the incarnation of the Son of God – his becoming a real human being for about thirty to thirty-five years on earth, and returning to heaven with a glorified human bodily existence. 'There is a Man in heaven!', one Scottish pastor used to love to proclaim from his pulpit. Unlike the Greek hope of the immortality of the soul, which was a popular pagan belief at the time, Peter taught the resurrection of the body as the ultimate future to which Christians should look forward, but argued that the purpose of Christian obedience in this life is the fleshing out of the implications of this future hope in the here and now. The ethics of Christian realism as based on the teaching of Jesus and his apostles must, therefore, always reflect this tension between already and not yet, and motivate believers towards more faithful attitudes and actions by challenging their convictions and commitments so that they may be increasingly resonant with what can best be termed the presence of the future.[3]

This might seem like theological gobbledegook, but it is really common sense! All of us who are professing Christians agree that we need continually to grow in our convictions and commitments, or our faith will vegetate. Yet many of us are called to follow Christ today in a Western world in which the majority of people are motivated by promises of success, satisfaction or freedom from stress entirely in the here and now. They criticize those who, as far as they are concerned, promise 'pie in the sky when you die', whether they be Christian, Islamic, or Jew. Perhaps our task in the twenty-first century Western world is even harder than that faced by Peter in first-century Asia Minor. At least there was a recognition of the validity of religious ideas in the culture which he sought to influence for Christ. It was pluralist, as there were many different forms of religious devotion from which to choose, and there was a degree of openness to new ideas and practices. In our culture, conformity to the cult of consumerism has become a real barrier to many who find it virtually impossible to consider that there may be more to life than meets the eye.

Exhortation and motivation

Lauri Thurén says that the main purpose of 1 Peter is to intensify the Christian conviction and commitment of people who are tempted to conform to the surrounding society in one way or another.[4] Peter is emphasizing that behaviour is indicative of faith, so that his statements about God, Christ, or redemption are used in order to produce right attitudes and good actions.[5] Thurén observes that Peter's audience is assumed to be already convinced, but not fully persuaded or adequately motivated, and that it is motivation which is Peter's main aim. He believes that if he can enhance right attitudes and encourage them to be more steadfast in their convictions, this will produce the desired outcome of changed behaviour and lifestyle.[6] Thurén emphasizes that this exhortation is not issued for its own sake, as something Peter feels duty bound to get off his chest (given his position as an apostle), or for him to further his educational, moralistic, or socializing purposes, but that 'The paraenesis was necessary for keeping the faith of the believers alive, and for making missionary activity possible by enhancing the credibility of the Christians.'[7]

This conclusion is important for our contemporary context if we have a concern for the current declining state of the churches, in much of the Western world at least. Ethical exhortation has become unfashionable as the result of years of abuse during which ethical imperatives, disconnected from the great theological indicatives, were often used from pulpits in an attempt to motivate congregations by guilt manipulation. I can recall sermons which I heard only twenty years ago, which were only very loosely connected with any biblical text, the objectives of which were to move hearers to feel compassion for the poor in the majority world and give more generously to provide aid of various kinds. In contrast to that kind of approach, 1 Peter recognizes that there is another dynamic at work when people are truly motivated to help the poor or engage in any other activity which is faithful to the call of Christ and carried out in his name. That means that people need power to act, and such power is available through Jesus Christ. Peter's paraenesis, therefore, brings power to the people! In this relatively short piece of writing, 1 Peter, we have an apostolic manifesto for true liberty for all God's people. Now that is one of the key points for our discussion of 'Lording It' and leading God's people, as we shall see later in this book.

Our first concern in this chapter is to help us understand the kind of argument which Peter uses in his letter as he tries to persuade his hearers to move on in their Christian faith and lifestyle. There's no rocket science here, but rather a very common sense approach which would have fitted in very well with their situation, and which makes sense for us today if we make an effort to understand the context. As we shall see, Peter's method and message are immediately relevant to the issues that we are seeking to address in this book. But what were his congregations' situations in first-century Asia Minor? It's not easy for us to transport ourselves back 2,000 years in time and imagine what life was really like for the average person in that part of the Roman Empire. Today we call that land Turkey, which has for centuries been a heartland of Islam. We find it strange that so many of the New Testament letters were sent to Christian churches scattered all over that sub-continental landmass. Yet John prefixed his Revelation with letters to seven significant churches in the province of Asia, including Ephesus, to which Paul had written Ephesians thirty years earlier at the same time as he wrote Colossians to a neighbouring city in Asia. Christianity was big-time in first-century 'Turkey', in other words, whereas today there are very few Christian believers in that country. For over 600 years some of the most important churches and Christian theologians were to be found in that great land, yet after the spread of Islam reached Asia Minor, a great change took place. If it is true that Muhammad's vision for the new religious movement, which he believed expressed real submission to the living God, was in part a reaction to a heretical brand of Monophysite (Christ-One-Nature) Christianity which was practised in seventh-century Arabia, it may be argued that there may well have been a similar situation in Cappadocia and the other former provinces of Asia Minor. If that is the case, then it means that the churches had lost touch with the paraenesis of Peter, at some time during those seven centuries, so that the practical message of 1 Peter had been largely forgotten.

Of course, that is a chilling reminder for those of us who live in countries like Scotland, which have known the light of the gospel for over 1,600 years. We may be at a point in our national history which is a defining moment, perhaps even a last chance, for us to turn back to God as a nation by putting into practice the preaching of Peter, Paul, and the other foundational teachers of the faith. A few years ago I worshipped in Greyfriars Kirk in Edinburgh, where the famous National Covenant was signed in 1638, a document that was, in effect, a declaration of spiritual independence by the majority of the people of Scotland who were committed Presbyterians and wished to remain so, despite King Charles I's clumsy attempts at imposing Episcopalian church order and government. Once that big building was bustling with two large congregations every Sunday. But today, relatively few faithful folk worship regularly in that famous parish kirk. As the churches in the two-thirds world grow apace, some observers believe that the net expansion of the Christian community worldwide exceeds 50,000 souls per day. Yet we are used to church shrink, rather than church growth, in most Western countries, apart from the US. So Peter's message may be far more important than we can even begin to imagine, and our response to his challenge about Christian leadership may be a determinative factor for the future flourishing of Christianity in many countries which have benefited from the gospel over the centuries. Following Peter's persuasive method and message, this digression is not intended to scare us into submission! Rather, it is to enable us to sense the urgency of our need to re-engage with the apostolic teachings which are the foundations of Christian faith and life for individuals, families and societies, so that we may be empowered to serve Christ with renewed vision and vigour, into the twenty-first century of the Christian Era and beyond.

Paroikoi – dispersed and different

What was life really like for believers in the first-century Roman provinces of what we now call Turkey? With what patterns of leadership would they have been familiar, in both civil society and religious communities? What did the rule of the Roman invaders really imply in terms of the ordering of daily life? What freedom did the people have to create the fabric of their family lives, community organizations and church fellowships, as conscience cried? Thankfully, New Testament scholars have not ignored the sociological dimension in seeking to understand the background to 1 Peter, and we must spend a little time exploring their findings, with the help of an important study by John Elliott.[8]

Elliott begins with a survey of the use of the concept of *paroikos*, 'resident alien', which is a key feature in the letter. The word, when used in Greco-Roman inscriptions and the Septuagint,[9] refers to 'strangers, foreigners, people who are not at home, or who lack native roots, in language, customs, culture, or political, social, and religious allegiances of the people among whom they dwell'.[10] Peter begins his letter by addressing his audience as *paroikoi*, 'exiles'. In modern parlance, the word and its cognates depict the displaced person who is viewed by the natives as a curious or suspicious-looking foreigner or stranger. It implies social separation, cultural alienation and some personal deprivation.[11] Usually, it has a specific political/legal meaning, referring to the condition, position, or fate of the resident alien, who is dwelling abroad without civil or nationality rights. In official lists of first-century city residents, *paroikoi* are ranked below full citizens and above strangers, freedmen and slaves. So they were not in the same plight as contemporary asylum seekers in the UK, for example, who are awaiting a decision about whether they can make this country their residence, and may be deported. They were recognized politically and registered as a stratum of the population which was distinguished legally and socially from full citizens, their superiors, and their inferiors, the transient foreigners. To gain the status of *paroikos* one had to have resided in a particular province for a certain period, or to have been granted, as a freedman or slave, a special dispensation by the state.

The advantages of being classed as a resident alien in the Roman Empire included, first of all, some political/legal recognition and potential upward social mobility for the underclass, landless and foreign elements in a province. Secondly, *paroikoi* did not have the same responsibilities as full citizens. However, there were certain disadvantages. First and foremost, they lacked the rights and privileges of *politai* (Roman citizens). Remember that Paul, when he was about to be sentenced to death for sedition, appealed to Caesar, as a Roman citizen of no ordinary city, Tarsus in Cilicia (Acts 21:39; 22:25–29). Resident aliens had no such right. Secondly, they were outsiders in terms of social interaction due to their origin, language, customs and religion. Thirdly, the status of resident alien meant political and economic exploitation, the disdain and suspicion of citizens, and competition and envy from those below them in the 'pile'.

Those readers of 1 Peter who were familiar with the Septuagint would immediately have understood the concept in context, from the stories, for example, of Abraham among the Hittites (Gen. 23:4), Moses in Midian (Ex. 2:22), and the Israelites in Egypt (1 Chron. 29:15). However, the patriarchal metanarrative, or big story, is clearly the main connection which Peter wants to make throughout the letter. Christians are called exiles (1 Pet. 1:1, 2:11) because that is how Abraham and his family were described, and many of the allusions made by Peter can be placed within the story of Abraham, Sarah, and their household. Peter's people have 'hope through the resurrection' (1:3, cf. Gen. 22:5,8,14; Heb. 11:19), yet they also share 'Grief in all kinds of trials' (1:6, cf. Gen. 22:1ff) in the same way as God tested Abraham, who was the father of the 'Apiru' or 'Hebrew', an Egyptian term of abuse for the displaced person/pastoral nomad (e.g. Gen. 14:13, Ex. 1:15). This appellation signifies a propertyless, dependent, immigrant, foreign social class rather than a specific ethnic group. In this way, Abraham confessed, 'I am a foreigner and stranger among you' (Gen. 23:4).

This concept was later elaborated in the Mosaic concern for the alien as a reflection of the character of the LORD, who 'defends the cause of the fatherless and the widow, and loves the foreigners residing among you, giving them food and clothing' (Deut. 10:18). The Hebrew word *ger/gerim* denotes a class of people who are landless but reside in Israel's land under the protection of certain families within Israel. In fact, the Israelites' status before the LORD as their supreme landlord, is as *gerim*. Christopher Wright notes: 'The moral character of Yahweh combines here . . . In some ancient near eastern royal texts the exaltation of national gods is commonly followed by the derivative exaltation of the royal household. But who . . . are the beneficiaries of Yahweh's supreme lordship? The fatherless, the widow, and the alien!'[12] 'Other gods have other ways, but Israel must "keep the way of the LORD", by doing what is right and just.'[13]

The exiled Jews in Babylon were called sons of *paroikia* in Ezra 8:35. We also know from the historian Josephus that the Seleucid (Syrian) King Antiochus III (226–187 BCE) transferred 2,000 Jewish families from Mesopotamia and Babylon to Phrygia in central Asia Minor.[14] So the Jews of the Diaspora[15] understood only too well what the designation *paroikos* meant for resident aliens in Roman times. In the Septuagint, the noun and its cognate verb are used over 100 times, most often to describe the situation and the political, legal and socio-religious conditions of Israelites living 'abroad' as resident aliens. Less frequently, it refers to aliens who lived among the Israelites in the Holy Land, who were restricted from participation in certain cultic rites and duties but still enjoyed some privileges of legal protection and social acceptance. Moses commanded the people in these terms: 'Do not despise an Egyptian, for you resided as foreigners in their country' (Deut. 23:7).

King David was also aware of the Israelites' historical status as strangers and aliens, even in the promised land: 'We are *paroikoi*, as were all our ancestors' (1 Chron. 29:15); and 'Everything comes from you, and we have given you only what comes from your hand' (1 Chron. 29:14), which compare with Psalm 39:12, 'I am a *paroikos* as all my ancestors were.' All of this speaks of David's personal identification with those who are dislocated, dispossessed and estranged, an identification that was carried through into spiritual significance.

In the New Testament, the concept is used five times in eight documents, which is not a great number of occurrences. Yet all are particularly pertinent. Two of them are in 1 Peter, and I shall expound them in detail below. The others are in Luke–Acts, Ephesians, and Hebrews, all of which are associated by some scholars, in some way, with Doctor Luke, the travelling companion of the apostle Paul. Luke–Acts, a two-volume defence of the faith dedicated to one 'Theophilus', makes up more than a quarter of the text of the New Testament, and in it Luke is revealed to be not only Christianity's first great historian, but also a theologian of remarkable insight. Some scholars have also noted possible connections with the letter to the Hebrews, because of linguistic and other similarities with Luke's Gospel and Acts. Luke was probably with Paul in Rome when he wrote Ephesians, as Paul records in Colossians 4:14, which was also probably written from Rome about the same time that 'Our dear friend Luke, the doctor' was with him, during his time of house arrest and imprisonment.

Luke also depicts Stephen's famous speech before the Sanhedrin, the Jewish Council in Jerusalem, in Acts 7, and twice Stephen speaks of their forefathers' experience as *paroikoi*. In Acts 7:6 he refers to Abraham's wanderings and the LORD's promise to him, 'Your descendants will be strangers in a country not their own . . .', and in 7:29 Stephen reminds his audience of Moses' flight to Midian, 'where he settled as a foreigner and had two sons'. It is significant that Paul, who witnessed that speech and was present as Stephen was stoned to death, was himself a Roman citizen and proud of it, because he knew the difference, sociologically as well as theologically, between a resident alien and a citizen. It is also worth noting that Luke was willing to give up his security, probably as a citizen, but at least as a *paroikos* of Antioch, the greatest city of the eastern Mediterranean at that time, in order to travel with Paul and spread the gospel. He also records the amazing fact, in Luke 24:18, that on the first Easter Sunday, after the resurrection, when Jesus appeared to two disciples on the road to Emmaus, they did not recognize him at first, and imagined him to be only a *paroikos*, telling him so. In a sense, that was revealing a theological truth which neither Cleopas nor his mate could possibly have intended to lay bare, in making such a derisory comment. Jesus is the *paroikos* par excellence, as we shall see later in this discussion.

Again, in Hebrews, the writer states, 'By faith Abraham lived as a *paroikos*' (Heb. 11:9), displaying a theologically nuanced understanding of the word, as did Paul in Ephesians 2:19, where he refers to Christians in the province of Asia as 'no longer *paroikoi* but fellow citizens'. In both cases, the writers are applying their appreciation of the plight of the resident alien to the actuality experienced by Christian pilgrims, who truly are journeying through foreign territory en route to their ultimate destination, the new heavens and earth yet to come. So when we come to 1 Peter, which was written by an author who probably knew the letter to the Ephesians, as I have argued in chapter 1, we wonder whether Peter is using the term *paroikos* entirely in its literal sense, or metaphorically, when he addresses his hearers as 'exiles' (1:1), exhorts them to 'Live out your time as foreigners here in reverent fear' (1:17), and urges them to abstain from sinful desires, 'as foreigners and exiles' (2:11). Were the Christians of

Asia Minor largely from the underclass, in other words, and was the gospel actually taking root among the poor? Or was this simply a powerful way of getting over the transitory nature of all things in this life, and thereby to teach the urgent necessity of getting one's priorities right as believers? Is it Peter's version of the famous passage in the Sermon on the Mount which climaxes with Jesus' famous dictum, 'Seek first his Kingdom and his righteousness, and all these things will be given to you as well' (Matt. 6:33)?

Elliott suggests that the term *paroikos* expresses, primarily, the real political/legal status and social conditions of the Christians' situation, as resident aliens in Asia Minor, affording, so Peter believed, a time of opportunity for them to get rid of ignorance in belief and futility in behaviour.[16] Elliott complains that recent English translations, among which we would include the popular NIV, have been inconsistent in the words chosen to translate *paroikos* and its cognates, with the result that the impression has been given that 1 Peter is focusing, primarily, on a pietistic hortatory message for spiritual pilgrims passing through this world, which contrasts present life on earth with future life in the world to come.

By definition, to be baptized as a Christian at that period in the eastern Roman Empire meant aligning oneself with the *paroikoi*, even if, like Paul, one retained and exercised one's Roman citizenship. As the gospel came first of all to the Jews, wherever the apostles preached, those who believed were sociologically connected with resident aliens. That was unavoidable, and part of the cost of discipleship for citizens. Legally, the status of Jews within the Empire, according to both Roman and local laws, involved restrictions regarding intermarriage, commercial interaction, property inheritance, land ownership, electoral rights, taxation, and the founding of associations, as well as making them susceptible to severer forms of civil and criminal punishment. 'For the Christian *paroikoi* of Asia Minor, like their Jewish counterparts in Alexandria, tenuous existence as resident aliens was fraught with profound and far-reaching political and socioeconomic as well as religious consequences . . . As the heirs of Abraham, Christians now share in the fateful history but also unique honour of the people of God.'[17]

Elliott argues convincingly that this terminology is used by Peter to describe social as well as religious circumstances. It is a question of both/and, rather than either/or, in other words.[18] This is a very important conclusion for the interpretation of 1 Peter, as we shall see, because we must seek to understand Peter's paraenesis in that social context – one of Christian communities which are set apart from and in tension with their social neighbours, rather than being assimilated and socially accepted. In fact, the temptation to conform and compromise was very real, and Peter, as a pastor full of compassion for his people, provides practical tools in his letter to enable ordinary Christians and their leaders to find renewed strength for the struggle of faith. For example, the 'sinful desires' (1 Pet. 2:11–12; 4:1–6), from which Christian resident aliens were to disentangle themselves, were typical of their lives before their conversion, and continued to be commonplace in the experience of many of their social neighbours. Christians must abstain from pagan vices because they spoil the witness of their exemplary conduct among the 'Gentiles' (a term which is used here in the special sense of 'non-Christians'). Elliott further reminds us that in the New Testament only the letter to the Hebrews has a sustained focus on the idea of the Christian life as pilgrimage, or preparation for the heavenly home.

Peter was clearly addressing a mixed audience of Jewish and Gentile Christians, which is understandable, given the cosmopolitan population of Asia Minor at the time, which, according to one recent estimate, included about 250,000 Jews as well as 5,000 Christians in a total population of about four million prior to 67 CE.[19] Church growth in the subsequent period of history was dramatic, especially in Asia Minor, and this could be partly attributed to the fact that, as in other regions, Christianity made its earliest and widest impact among Jewish converts and former pagan proselytes to Judaism. Because of this, Elliott argues that we need to be careful in our translation of *paroikos* and cognates, and related terminology. The noun *paroikia* should be rendered 'alien residence', *paroikos* as 'resident alien', and *parepidemoi* as 'visiting strangers', he concludes.

These terms depict the addressees of 1 Peter as an admixture of permanent and temporary strangers and aliens, some of whom are residing permanently in the five regions or four provinces of Asia Minor. Living under conditions of estrangement and socio-religious alienation in the 'diaspora' and 'Babylon' analogous to their Israelite forebears, the addressees and authors[20] share in a certain sense the predicaments as well as the hope of God's special elect and holy people.[21]

In this way, Christian resident aliens may well have been numbered with the rural population and villagers who had been relocated to urban areas and given an inferior status to citizens, being included among immigrant labourers, skilled workers, merchants, and traders, who either lived permanently in, or regularly travelled through, the eastern Empire. They were in a very real situation of actual social and religious estrangement and alienation, in other words. Their chief concern was the interaction of Christians in pagan society, and the various social distinctions and disagreements which had created a crisis for the growing Christian movement in Asia Minor. In view of this crisis, the apostolic team of writers who penned this circular letter which we now call 1 Peter, had a clear strategy, noted above. It was focused on the motivation of the communal self-consciousness of believers scattered across Asia Minor, and to mobilize their sense of solidarity and determination to persevere in faith, by appealing to them as those who had received the gracious love of a Father, from whom all fatherhood is named,[22] so that they had been adopted as honoured members of the household (*oikia*) of God.

Paternalism – not our pattern

From Augustus on, the Caesars exploited the patronage of the aristocratic families (*oikoi*), and personal loyalty to the Emperor was sought from all sections of the population, in the form of a personal oath of allegiance. Such loyalty was rewarded in imperial appointments, favours, or bequests. It also had a price tag. Subjects who pledged their loyalty to the Emperor as 'Father of the fatherland' submitted to a more universal claim to power.[23] This type of paternalism displays the emotional basis upon which the Lordship of the Caesars was built, and it meant that, with such a father as king, the Emperor's government was considered to be his extended family, and was given the title 'Caesar's Household'. With this came notions of the Empire as a commonwealth, with Caesar as head of a multinational family. This was reflected in the governance of the provinces, as we can see from this quotation from Pliny, the Roman governor of Bithynia-Pontus in Asia Minor, early in the second century CE, in which he refers to the significance of being included in his own household. Here he speaks of his domestic duties in acting as legal executor, even for his slaves: 'I receive and obey their last requests, as so many authoritative commands, suffering them to dispose of their effects to whom they please; with this single restriction, that they leave them to some of my household, for to persons in their station the household takes the place of city and commonwealth.'[24] This shows us the traditional pattern of household organization and management which was current thirty or forty years after 1 Peter was circulated in that region, and is an important clue to the social context of the letter, and the significance of the key theme of the household of God.

It is clear from writings of this period that there was a craving for some meaningful form of social existence and interaction which was wider than the nuclear or extended family, and narrower than the Roman state, the household of Caesar. Because of that there was a growth of voluntary associations, such as artisans' and tradespeople's guilds, to enhance social solidarity, and this was particularly attractive to displaced persons and asylum seekers. Guild members often lived and worked together, sharing the same housing blocks, so that they, too, considered their guild to be a household. They provided a social metaphor which the first Christians appreciated and, to a certain extent, adopted. For these Christians, too, were 'homeless people looking for a home', as were other religious groups which conceived of their communities as constituting a household, or family.[25] But, of course, the Christians of Asia Minor also knew, through their Jewish roots and branches, that this metaphor was a well-established biblical way of referring to the household of God's people. In the Septuagint *oikos* is found over 2,000 times, and *oikia* over 200 times. Notable examples are found in Exodus 13:3,14, when

Moses said that God had delivered the Israelites from the 'house of bondage' in Egypt, meaning the oppressive regime of Pharaoh. Again, in Exodus 19:3–6, Moses is depicted speaking to the Israelites at Mount Sinai before he receives the Ten Commandments from the LORD: 'Then Moses went up to God, and the LORD called to him from the mountain and said, "This is what you are to say to the house of Jacob and what you are to tell the people of Israel: You yourselves have seen what I did in Egypt, and how I carried you on eagles' wings and brought you to myself. Now if you obey me fully and keep my covenant, then out of all nations you will be my treasured possession. Although the whole earth is mine, you will be for me a kingdom of priests and a holy nation. These are the words you are to speak to the Israelites."' Peter uses these concepts in 1 Peter 2:4–5, where Christians are described as 'living stones, being built into a spiritual house, to be a holy priesthood, offering spiritual sacrifices acceptable to God through Jesus Christ'. Again, in 2:9–10, Peter says, 'You are a chosen people, a royal priesthood, a holy nation, God's special possession . . . Once you were not a people, but now you are the people of God.' It was this sense of, and longing for, belonging which was essential to their positive reception of the gospel: 'Christianity forged its way into secular society through individual household communities as the basic unit of its mission . . . Households (*oikiai*) constituted the focus, locus and nucleus of the ministry and mission of the Christian movement.'[26]

It was in those regions which were influenced by Hellenistic Roman culture, that the Christian movement had to reckon with the predominant position of the *paterfamilias* ('father of the family') and his huge influence both in civil society and over his own extended family, and determine how that might be viewed as an opportunity to promote and unfold their message as it was realized in pagan society. After all, Christians proclaimed and prayed to God as 'our Father', rather than adopting pagan spiritual forms of filial piety which were popular at the time. The concept of the household of God was certainly adopted as an all-embracing image of the entire believing community, and one of the key features of contemporary human households was subordination to those in authority, within a patriarchal order. This meant that seniority was greatly valued in the Christian communities, so that when 'elders' were appointed in each congregation, they were usually to be people of considerable Christian experience and committed to Christian service. *Presbyteros* ('elder') can mean both one of advanced age and somebody who has special responsibilities. But, as age conferred status and eligibility for leadership, there is no doubt that many of the first Christian leaders were also heads of families, that their households became Christian when they were converted, and that their homes became gathering places for believers. For this reason there are a number of greetings in New Testament letters which refer to key Christian households as leadership bases in the apostolic mission and ministries.

But what shape did this new form of 'paternalism' take, if indeed that is an appropriate description of the phenomena? Did Christian leaders merely copy the leadership styles which were broadly typical of the *paterfamilias* of Roman households or of the heads of Jewish families and elders of the synagogues?

There are some very crucial clues in the New Testament which can help us to answer these key questions. For example, Luke tells us in Acts 18:1–3 that when Paul arrived in Corinth, he met Aquila, from Pontus, who had recently arrived from Italy with his wife Priscilla because of Emperor Claudius's edict that excluded all Jews from the city of Rome. They, like Paul, were tentmakers by trade, so Paul not only lived with them in their home, he also shared in their day job for a period of about eighteen months (Acts 18:11), during which time a great evangelistic work was done, led by these three key members of the apostolic team. Crispus, the chief elder of the Jewish synagogue, believed in the Lord, together with his entire household, and, along with many other Corinthians, they were baptized as Christians (Acts 18:8). After this extended time of mission, Paul sailed across the Aegean Sea to the port of Ephesus, taking Priscilla and Aquila along with him. So it was that, in 1 Corinthians 16:19, Paul wrote from Ephesus to Corinth: 'The churches in the province of Asia send you greetings, Aquila and Priscilla greet you warmly in the Lord, and so does the church that meets at their house.' Aquila and Priscilla were then left in charge of the work in the capital city of the province of Asia, as Paul quickly returned to mission headquarters in Antioch of Syria (Acts 18:18–22). During their

leadership of the church in Ephesus, Priscilla and Aquila encoun-
tered an Alexandrian Jew called Apollos, who had evidently
received instruction in the Christian way, so that he was able to
preach boldly about Jesus. However, his theology was rather
incomplete, as he knew only the introductory message focused on
the call to repentance which had been associated with the ministry
of John the Baptist. Priscilla and Aquila therefore invited him to
their home and explained the way of God more adequately to
him, so that he was able to travel over to Greece and preach effectively in public debates with the Jews, proving from the Scriptures
that Jesus is the Christ (Acts 18:24–28). Following their spell of
service in Ephesus the couple were able to return to Rome after
the death of Claudius. When Paul wrote to the Roman church
during his second visit to Corinth two years after he had left his
colleagues in Ephesus, he said, 'Greet Priscilla and Aquila, my co-
workers in Christ Jesus. They risked their lives for me. Not only I
but all the churches of the Gentiles are grateful to them' (Rom.
16:3).

It is very significant that both Luke and Paul, the most prolific
Christian writers of the early church, should single out Aquila and
Priscilla as examples of Christian leadership and commend their
joint ministry so warmly to the catholic church. It is clear that Paul
regarded them as key co-workers, to whom he entrusted strategic
leadership in the city of Ephesus and its vast hinterland. Their
home and household were the base of that operation and oversight. They were, therefore, the leading *presbyteroi* (elders) or
episkopoi (overseers)[27] of the Ephesian church which gathered in
house meetings throughout the city and its environs. That Luke
and Paul, with their Hellenistic background and Jewish connections, could have calmly reported such a shocking fact in their circulated writings makes us realize that the early Christians were by
no means mimicking the traditional patterns of leadership which
were typical of the cultures within the eastern Empire. No woman
could have aspired to eldership in the Jewish synagogue, and in
fact, women were physically separated from men in their worship. Female leadership was recognized in the Jewish home, as
Proverbs 31:10–31 indicates. The homemaker is depicted there as
a woman of substance who engages not only in management of
the household, but also in matters of property and business. But

she did so under the headship of her husband, and we will return to that important concept later in our discussion.

As we have seen from our extended treatment of the household (*oikia*) in Greco-Roman cultures typical of the eastern Empire towards the end of the first century CE, it was culturally distinctive and radically original for a woman to take on the kind of leadership which was clearly assumed by Priscilla along with her husband Aquila, on equal terms, with the direction of the apostle Paul. Women could be overseers as well as deacons in the leadership structure of the early house churches, with the commendation of the apostles themselves. It is with this conclusion, which may be disturbing for some, that we close this chapter.[28]

Whatever 'not lording it' may have meant for Peter, it could not have implied the correction of men who had gone over the top and needed to adopt leadership styles more resonant with the kind of male-dominated and paternalistic patterns which were current in Asia Minor at the time. In fact, as we noted at the beginning of this chapter, it is more likely that Peter was seeking to motivate leaders to avoid assimilation with cultural patterns, and paternalism must have been high on his hit list. 'Lording it' is singled out by Peter as a quite distinctive problem, and I believe that it is just as destructive of healthy Christian fellowship in the twenty-first century as it was in the first, as I shall seek to explain and apply in the course of this book.[29] We shall try to follow Peter in his concern to avoid inappropriate ways of leading in the churches, especially those which are wedded to insights and influences that are not rooted in biblical models and tend uncritically to mimic imported cultural patterns, even when they arise from dominant sources such as ancient Rome or contemporary America, with their attendant control of much of the communication media.

Summary

Let's summarize where our discussion has taken us in chapter 3:

- We've understood 1 Peter to be a circular letter containing ethical exhortation, for the most part, expressing the concern of

Peter, Silas and Mark, who are writing from Rome to churches all over Asia Minor. They want to motivate Christians there, so that their faith is revitalized, and their outreach stimulated, by affirming the great truths of the faith and the ethical implications which ensue, while dealing with evils which the believers have tolerated and which are weakening their witness.

- We've learned that, like the Jewish communities from which many of them originated, many of the Christians in Asia Minor were resident aliens rather than Roman citizens. This involved a real stigma, which caused problems for Christians, both socially and religiously. It is a mistake to interpret the language of alienation as referring only to spiritual pilgrimage.

- We've also recognized the important place which the household had in the cultures of the eastern Empire in the late first century CE, and how leadership patterns from that context must have influenced the developing of styles of superintendence within the Christian communities. However, we have noted that, rather than copying the paternalistic, male only leadership models which were common in both Roman and Jewish societies, the apostles adopted a radically different approach, and included women in their leadership teams.

4

Elders and Shepherds

We have noted that the Romans normally tolerated non-Roman religious practices within the Empire, but that Judaism and associated sects, while often enjoying the protection of the state, were occasionally singled out for opprobrium. Julius Caesar (*c.* 50 BCE) had granted certain privileges to Jews for the practice of their religion, which were continued under successive emperors until Claudius (*c.* 50 CE), whose clampdown on Jewish meetings eventually led to a ban of Jews from Rome (*c.* 59 CE), which was mentioned in chapter 3. However, there was a Roman distaste for the practices of Judaism, and Tiberius, for example, at one point banished large numbers of Jews. Even after the Jewish revolt of 66–70 CE, culminating in the destruction of the Jerusalem temple, Vespasian and Titus continued certain privileges to Judaism, despite the heavy taxation which was levied specifically on the Jews. The Jews' religious exclusivity was the cause of much Roman distaste for their religion, and this was transferred to Christianity. However, the basic attitude of tolerance was also applied to the Christian faith.[1] There were a number of non-religious organized groups or societies which were tolerated under successive Roman imperial regimes. They were voluntary associations of individuals who wanted to pursue some common interest, whether cultural, commercial, or sporting, to name but a few categories. Such groups attracted large numbers of members, and were subject to official scrutiny, both when they were first established and during their development. The most common were professional groups and religious burial societies, but there is little evidence to suggest that many needed, or were given, official permission to exist at the time 1 Peter was written. As early as the second century BCE, however, attempts were made to control these organizations, and sometimes only those with an ancient pedigree escaped an imperial ban. Pliny, when governor of Bithynia-Pontus, corresponded with the Emperor Trajan about Christian congregations in Asia Minor, but this probably had more to do with Trajan's concerns about the power of voluntary societies, rather than being a sign of any growing intolerance towards Christianity. In fact, it is likely that the earliest recorded confrontations between church and state were the result of the fact that, to the Romans, Christian congregations seemed more like voluntary societies rather than organized religious groups.[2]

That is an interesting insight for our discussion of our key passage in 1 Peter 5:1–5. We have noted that the authors' aim in writing this circular from Rome to the scattered congregations in Asia Minor was to maintain the distinctive witness of the Christian communities and to discourage assimilation with the pagan culture around. If there was some confusion among the authorities about the difference between Christian groups and other voluntary associations, it is certain that patterns of leadership would have been a key factor. Christian leaders would have to account for their distinctive beliefs and practices, yet would also want to benefit from the broadly tolerant attitudes of their overlords when that did not conflict with their self-awareness as members of the household of God. That is why we see deference advocated in 1 Peter to those who exercise proper civil authority: 'Submit yourselves for the Lord's sake to every human authority: whether to the emperor, as the supreme authority, or to governors, who are sent by him to punish those who do wrong and to commend those who do right . . . Show proper respect to everyone . . . honour the emperor' (2:13–17).

Peter, Mark, and Rome

Yet there was bound to be conflict between the developing ideology of Christianity and the growth of the imperial cult, which only became official policy in the third century CE, when Emperor Decius demanded universal adherence to a political loyalty oath as well as to the worship of the emperor as divine. Pliny referred to this subject in his correspondence with Trajan as early as *c.* 110:

> Others whose names were given to me by the informer, first admitted the charge and then denied it; they said they had ceased to be Christians two or more years previously, and some of them even twenty years ago. They all did reverence to your statue and the images of the gods in the same way as the others, and reviled the name of Christ . . . they had met regularly before dawn on a fixed day to chant verses alternatively among themselves in honour of Christ as if to a god, and also to bind themselves by oath, not for any criminal purpose, but to abstain from theft, robbery and adultery, to commit no breach of trust and not to deny a deposit when called upon to restore it. After this ceremony it had been their custom to disperse and reassemble later to take food of an ordinary, harmless kind; but they had in fact given up this practice since my edict, issued on your instructions, which banned all political societies.

Trajan replied, approving of Pliny's approach:

> You have followed the right course of procedure in your examination of the cases of persons charged with being Christians, for it is impossible to lay down a general rule to a fixed formula.[3]

The Romans, however, distinguished between worshipping a god (Latin *deus*) and revering a divine emperor (*divus*), in the latter part of the first century, during which 1 Peter was written and circulated. Different emperors had various attitudes to the practice of according divine honours to themselves, and the extent to which they permitted or required personal religious obeisance. Participation in the cult was more important in provincial Asia Minor than in Rome. The historian Tacitus tells us that in Rome the emperor was revered as divine only after his death. However, it was a different story in Asia Minor. All the emperors of the first century CE, from Augustus to Domitian, had divine honours attributed to them, and temples to Vespasian and Titus were erected in Asia Minor. This was a convenient way for certain cities to demonstrate their loyalty to the Empire, and in some

provincial situations it actually provided a culturally approved
cultic way of accounting for their acceptance of subjugation to
Rome. The cult of the divine emperor tended not to continue long
after that emperor's death, and flourished in order to maintain
cultural stability and control in the provinces.[4]

In this way, cultic reverence for Rome and the emperor perme-
ated the entire culture of the Hellenistic cities of Asia Minor, so
that any challenge to the imperial cult would have been perceived as a challenge not only to Roman rule, but also to the
social and cultural fabric itself. Conformity was therefore expected by the local authorities more so than by the Roman overlords,
and this was signified in terms of pressure to conform to social
expectations rather than by the enforcing of specific political or
religious beliefs. That is a key factor in our interpretation of the
particular pressures, which Peter speaks about in this letter. It is
also important for our understanding of the idea of 'lording it',
and the prohibition attached to that leadership style by the apostolic team. So let's look a little more closely at 1 Peter 5:1–5:

> To any elders among you, therefore, I appeal as fellow-elder and
> witness to the sufferings of Christ, and a sharer as well in the glory
> to be revealed: Shepherd the flock of God that is in your care.
> Watch over it not out of compulsion but willingly before God, not
> greedily but with enthusiasm. Don't lord it over your respective
> congregations, but be examples to the flock, and when the chief
> shepherd appears you will receive the unfading crown of glory.
> You in turn who are younger must defer to the authority of elders.
> All of you with each other, then, clothe yourselves with humility,
> for God opposes the arrogant, but gives grace to the humble.[5]

This caution against overbearing leadership would have originated, in Peter's thinking, with the teaching of Jesus recorded in
Mark 10:42–44, where Christ rebukes James and John for asking
that they sit on his right and left in his glorious kingdom and then
calls the twelve together, saying:

> You know that those who are regarded as rulers of the Gentiles
> lord it over them, and their high officials exercise authority over
> them. Not so with you. Instead, whoever wants to become great

among you must be your servant, and whoever wants to be first must be slave of all. For even the Son of Man did not come to be served but to serve, and to give his life as a ransom for many.[6]

Mark and Peter were, therefore, concerned to apply the dominical teaching about the potential abuse of leadership positions within the Christian communities in this context, and we should not view 1 Peter 5:1–5 as laying down guidelines about the qualities and qualifications required of Christian leaders. Paul's instructions to Timothy and Titus concerning the appointment of overseers/elders would have been well known in the Asian churches, at least, and certainly in Rome, where 1 Peter originated. Here, Mark and Peter are focusing on what not to do: 'Watch over the flock not out of compulsion . . . not greedily . . . not lording it . . . not arrogant.'

Elders are ministers – male and female

Peter calls himself a 'fellow elder' rather than an apostle, in this exhortation, because he wants to identify with the church leaders and share his sense of solidarity with them.[7] That was a key part of his rhetorical strategy, the way we set about trying to persuade and motivate others through the skilful use of words. He doesn't pull rank on them, as a superior to inferiors, in other words, although he might have tried that approach. Paul did so in his disagreements with the Corinthians, some of whom had questioned his apostolic authority, when he responded, 'I persevered in demonstrating among you the marks of a true apostle, including signs, wonders, and miracles' (2 Cor. 12:12). Earlier Paul had used the rhetorical questions, 'Am I not an apostle? Have I not seen Jesus our Lord?' (1 Cor. 9:1). Obviously, Peter's status as an eyewitness of the resurrection was not in question, as he had been among the first to hear the good news and meet the risen Christ on the first Easter Sunday. He had also been the first to preach the full gospel to the multitude in Jerusalem, on the Day of Pentecost, following the outpouring of the Holy Spirit, a crowd which had included Jewish proselytes from the very provinces in which 1 Peter's addressees lived, some of whom had doubtless returned to persuade their friends in the synagogues that the Messiah had come. Given his position, then, he could have pulled rank, but he chose a tactic which was in harmony with his purpose. He was actually demonstrating the truth he wanted to convey. He was preaching what he practised, and practising what he preached. The Lord had taught him not to be overbearing, and that was not something which would have come easily to Peter, from what we know of his natural bearing in the Gospels.

Why were church leaders called elders? We noted in chapter 3 that both the Roman *paterfamilias* and the Jewish synagogue ruler (elder) were dominant figures in the cultures of Asia Minor at the time, and that seniority was greatly valued, as it is in many Eastern cultures today. This is in contrast with contemporary Western cultures, which tend to value the vision and energy of youth more highly than the wisdom and experience of old age, attributes which were then considered to be essential to effective leadership and which were more likely to be found in older persons. But remember that in those days anybody over forty years of age was considered quite old, and that life expectancy was much lower than today. Peter was literally 'an older man' (*presbyteros*), and was probably in his sixties when he wrote from Rome, as he had been church-planting in the Empire for over thirty years. It is significant that we know very little about his activities in Asia Minor, apart from what we can glean from 1 and 2 Peter, because Luke's account in Acts majors on the missionary travels of Paul. The last we hear of Peter in Luke's story of Christian origins is in Acts 15:7–11, where Peter addresses the apostles and elders of the church at the Council of Jerusalem about the vexed question of the full inclusion of non-Jews into the church. Luke tells us that in response to Peter's speech 'Then the apostles and elders, with the whole church, decided to choose some of their own men and send them to Antioch with Paul and Barnabas' (15:22).

So from the beginning the elders acted with the apostles and the whole church when making and implementing decisions. If that was true about a momentous decision like the recognition of Gentiles within the Christian fold, it was also to be reflected in the normal, day-to-day oversight of congregations. Elders were not to act as plenipotentiaries of the apostles, nor were they to dominate the other church members. The problem was that there were some elders who were domineering, in that sense, and that is still true today. They may give the impression that they are but the mouthpieces of the apostles, or they may set themselves up as independent authorities, as some had done in Corinth, claiming to know better than Paul. That is why Peter takes the trouble to deal with the issue of 'lording it'. Then, as now, authoritarianism was a real problem.

Today, 'bishop', 'priest', 'pastor' or 'minister' may be the title given to those who are in charge of most congregations, within the various Christian traditions, and 'elder' may more often be used as the name for those leaders who serve as deacons did in New Testament times. Paul addresses the overseers (elders) and deacons of the church at Philippi as forming the corporate leadership of the church (Phil. 1:1). He also instructs Timothy about the qualifications required by male and female deacons (1 Tim. 3:8–13). This distinction between deacons and elders is recognized by Peter in 1 Peter 4:11, where he distinguishes between those leaders who speak and those who serve.[8] From the beginning, the apostles concentrated on prayer and the ministry of preaching, and they delegated the practical care of the congregations, especially of the widows and the needy, to seven others, all of whom had Greek names (Acts 6:1ff). Although those seven were not the archetypal deacons, that pattern, it seems, became a model for the Christian congregations which the apostles planted as the movement spread north into Syria and Cilicia, and then into Asia Minor.

Clearly, the original apostles retained a distinctive and formative role in the whole church. Through them and their associates, the message was clarified and formulated, communicated and inscripturated. But they did not act either independently, or in concert with fellow apostles, as monarchical bishops or as a college of bishops. The pattern of the monarchical episcopate seems to have emerged in the early second century due to a failure to reckon with what Peter clearly teaches in this key text in 1 Peter 5:1–5. For example, in 115 CE, Ignatius of Smyrna could command his people to 'Do nothing without the bishop', which seems very different in approach from what Peter was directing fifty years earlier.

Peter simply exhorts elders to tend God's flock, as good shepherds, and as followers of the Chief Shepherd, who had suffered for the sheep. This imagery is rooted in the Old Testament tradition which describes God as the shepherd of his people Israel, and is most profoundly expressed by David in Psalm 23 when he confesses, 'The LORD is my shepherd', a confession that arose out of his own experience as a shepherd and the dangers which he daily faced in order to provide for and guide his flock. Similar imagery was taken up by Jesus in his parable of the lost sheep (Mt. 18:12–14), where the punchline is 'In the same way your Father in heaven is not willing that any of these little ones should perish.' The care and courage of the good shepherd is but a reflection of the characteristics of the Chief Shepherd, who has become human in Jesus Christ, who suffered and died so that the flock might be gathered in, provided for on the way, and guided towards their ultimate destination. He has no wish for any of the flock to be lost, and so has appointed under-shepherds to take care of them.

Peter himself had received a special calling to feed God's sheep, you will recall, after the resurrection of Jesus, as John tells us in John 21:16ff. Three times in that passage the risen Lord asked Peter to reverse his earlier denial by affirming his love for Christ, and three times he commanded him to take care of his flock by feeding them. As Moses had explained that 'people do not live on bread alone, but on every word that comes from the mouth of the LORD' (Deut. 8:3), Peter understood what his task was from then on. Elder-shepherds are primarily teachers of God's word. That is why the terminology is confusing for some of us within the Reformed churches, which have adopted the title 'elder' for church leaders who are not called to teach and preach. It is very dangerous to assume that the modern appellation 'elder' is anything like the use of the Greek word *presbyteros* in New Testament times! For Peter, 'elder' was equivalent to 'minister of the word' in the Presbyterian tradition,[9] 'pastor' in the Baptist tradition, and 'priest' or 'bishop' in Anglican, Roman Catholic or Orthodox communions.

This understanding of the term elder is further demonstrated by the fact that Peter, like Paul, uses elder and overseer interchangeably. We saw how Paul directed Titus concerning the ordaining of elders in Crete and spoke of them in the same breath as overseers. The former focuses on their seniority and responsibility, and the latter on the task at hand. Elders are what these leaders are, and overseeing is what they do, in other words. So Peter, the fellow elder, exhorts elders to take care of the flock (1 Pet. 5:1), by exercising oversight (5:2). In the Church of Scotland, ministers are inducted to a charge, which may consist of one or more parish churches. That practice is rooted in this Petrine passage, and reflects Peter's own 'induction' to his ministry after the resurrection appearance of Christ by the Sea of Galilee. The oversight is exercised through the feeding and guiding of the flock by the word of God, in other words. The elder, according to Peter, is supremely the servant of the Lord's word, and the same cluster of words is also found in Paul's speech to the Ephesian elders in Acts 20:28: 'Keep watch over yourselves and all the flock, of which the Holy Spirit has made you overseers. Be shepherds of the church of God, which he bought with his own blood.' But then Paul went on to prepare them for the task ahead, which included protecting the people from false teachers: 'I know that after I leave, savage wolves will come in among you and will not spare the flock. Even from your own number men will arise and distort the truth in order to draw away disciples after them. So be on your guard!' (20:29–31)

New Testament 'elders', as ministers of God's word, and as guides and guardians of God's people, exercising faithfully their oversight of the church of God, must prepare believers to discern the difference between good and bad shepherds, in other words. There will be leaders who are chosen from the membership who are out for their own ends, and who twist the truth to suit the likings of their hearers and thus try to control them for their own purposes of self-aggrandizement and/or empire-building. In Paul's famous last words to Timothy, he said virtually the same thing:

> I give you this charge: Preach the word; be prepared in season and out of season; correct, rebuke, and encourage – with great patience and careful instruction. For the time will come when people will not put up with sound doctrine. Instead, to suit their own desires, they will gather around them a great number of teachers to say what their itching ears want to hear' (2 Tim. 4:1–3).

The distinction between good and bad shepherds is brought out by Peter's use of two words which he and/or Silas seem to have created especially for this discussion, as they are not found in Greek prior to the period during which 1 Peter was probably completed. The first is *allotriepiskopos*, found in 1 Peter 4:15, and the second is *sympresbyteros*, found in 5:1. The former occurs towards the end of a section on persecution and suffering: Christians (especially leaders) are told to expect that, and are warned not to bring on suffering for the wrong reasons. One such cause is what we would call 'meddling in the affairs of others'. The word *allotriepiskopos* literally means the exercising of inappropriate oversight over others, so applies particularly to those who are recognized as elders/overseers. There have been concerns about heavy-handed shepherding in some of the new church movements during the past thirty years or so, but traditional denominations are by no means free of such negative influences. Such pastors try to lead the church by domineering, 'intruding into an alien sphere of office'.[10] In contrast, there are those who gladly embrace the second reference, and are happy to be 'fellow-elders' like Peter. They reject notions of individualistic assertion of their powers of oversight, and conduct themselves as team members who share the responsibility of leadership, and do not ask of other pastors any more than they ask of themselves. *Sympresbyteros* is a statement of solidarity, and quite the opposite of the interfering approach of the *allotriepiskopos*.

Peter has, as one would expect in the light of our discussion in chapter 2, more detail about the proper motivation which good shepherds should have in order to ensure that they set about their task in the way of Christ and his apostles. He uses three pairs of contrasting phrases in 5:2b–3: 'not under pressure but willingly, not because of any stipend but eagerly, not by harsh command but by example'.[11] These are all set within the context of suffering, as 5:1 indicates. The true shepherd is willing to sacrifice a great deal for the good of his or her flock, and there will be many struggles, both external and internal: 'conflicts on the outside, fears within', as Paul honestly remarked (2 Cor. 7:5). That means that ministers/priests/pastors should expect hassle, as par for the course. They should not be surprised by the surfacing of internal disputes which will often spoil congregational life and witness for a time, or by the onset of persecution by hostile individuals and group-ings in the, as yet, non-Christian community. They are to exercise their leadership duties without coercion, which implies that they all have choices in the matter, and have themselves been chosen, yet are called to carry out the will of God rather than simply being enthusiastic about what they do. They are not to be motivated by monetary matters, although they have a right to be supported adequately by their congregations, as Paul says in 1 Corinthians 9:7–12, culminating with, 'If others have this right of support from you, shouldn't we have it all the more?' It is as if Peter is building up to a crescendo of challenge to the leaders of the churches of Asia Minor. Then comes the punchline, in the third antithesis: 'Not as those who lord it over their underlings, but as those who become examples for the flock' (5:3). The remainder of this chap-ter will be devoted to an exposition of this verse.

Not lording it

An eminent New Testament scholar once described the first com-ing of Christ as a language event, by which he meant that many old Greek words took on new Hebrew meanings, and other words were created to carry the special concepts and definitions which the teaching of Jesus and his apostles entailed. We've seen one such new word in *sympresbyteros*, 'fellow-elder', in 1 Peter 5:1, a term which Peter himself seems to have coined, as it does not appear in Greek literature prior to the writing and circulation of this letter. The use of the compound verb *katakyrieuein*, trans-lated 'to lord it over', recalls Jesus' warning to his disciples in Mark 10:42, as we have noted above, where the context is also that of servant-leader behaviour of Christian leaders in contrast with that of secular authorities, as we have noted in his advo-cacy of deference in 1 Peter 2:13–17.[12] This verb occurs eighteen times in the Septuagint, often meaning 'to subjugate an enemy' or 'to rule by force over unwilling subjects'.[13] The probable meaning here is that elders 'are not to exercise their power for themselves and therewith against those entrusted to them'.[14]

But that assumes that we understand the significance of the part of the verb which derives from the noun *kyrios*, 'lord'. After all, we live in an age when the concepts of the divine right of kings, and autocratic monarchy, have long been consigned to the history books, following the disastrous clash of empires which led to the World Wars of the first half of the twentieth century. Our Queen in the United Kingdom is a constitutional monarch who dares not attempt to reign without the concurrence of Parliament, unlike her ill-fated forebear, King Charles I, who literally lost his head in pursuing his convictions about the rightful powers of royalty and in so doing dissolved Parliament, on more than one occasion, when it suited his cause. We might say that Charles learned the hard way about the perils of lording it! But is there any real danger that Christian ministers, pastors, or priests might adopt a similar attitude in the twenty-first century, and try to rule their congregations, dioceses, or even whole denominations, by such methods? Some Protestants might immediately point the finger at Roman Catholics, who continue to appoint 'Cardinal Archbishops', at the behest of the Pope, and often refer to them as 'Princes of the Church'. That seems to hark back to the days when the Papal States were a very real political force in Italy, and when the Pope appointed and crowned the Holy Roman Emperor, who ruled over large swathes of Europe. I was therefore amazed, when I first met the Roman Catholic Archbishop of St Andrews and Edinburgh during my service as the full-time ecumenical chaplain to a technological university, that he introduced himself to me and invited me to call him by his first name! 'Call me Keith,' said Keith Patrick O'Brien, with a warm smile, and so I have done, ever since. However, I immediately noticed that Catholics from his diocese were unlikely to share my new-found liberty. In my hearing, most of them addressed Keith as 'Your grace', and some kissed his archiepiscopal ring. Recently, many of us in Scotland's churches shared the joy of our Roman Catholic brothers and sisters when Keith O'Brien was awarded the red beretta and elevated, by the Pope, to the office of Cardinal, in Rome. We have read the moving testimonies of fellow clergy who know Keith to be a down-to-earth and humble servant of the Lord. Yet we Presbyterian ministers would never dream of treating him as anything other than an equal before God, and certainly not as royalty![15]

However, we don't have to travel too far from Scotland, or in Scotland, to recognize examples of Protestant leaders who expect and receive the kind of obeisance and deference of which they are often so critical in the Roman church. One only has to observe the influence and power which is wielded by the Revd Dr Ian Paisley in Northern Ireland, for example, both within his Free Presbyterian Church of Ulster denomination, and through his political party, the Democratic Unionists.

In my lifetime, post-World War II, I can recall other ecclesiastical figures who have 'lorded it' in a big way. In my first year as an ordained minister I attended the 1978 General Assembly, when the Moderator, the Revd Dr Peter Brodie, presented, so he thought, a watertight case for the union of the Church of Scotland with Scottish Methodists. I remember his powerful rhetoric, which persuaded the Assembly unanimously to approve the proposal of his committee, and the tumultuous applause which resulted. However, the next day our brethren, in their Methodist Conference, decided to throw out the proposals! And one of the stated reasons was that they feared they would be swallowed up by their sister church, like a company which is taken over by a larger rival. They may well have been right, and the Methodist Church in Scotland continues to make a distinctive witness, despite their relatively few congregations, in comparison with south of the border.

Then, we cannot forget the testimony of the Independent churches and assemblies in Scotland, which I have come to know well over the years. Members of the Christian Brethren, for example, are proud of their traditions, which go back to the early nineteenth century, among which is that they do not usually employ stipendiary pastors to oversee their fellowships. In some assemblies that is changing, and evangelists, youth workers, and pastors are being called to serve full-time or part-time. Yet they still maintain the tradition of being led by elders, who share in the work of preaching and leading worship. In that way, they believe that they are closer to the New Testament tradition of the 'tent-maker', who has a day job and devotes his spare time to Christian service. Yet there have been notable examples of certain elders who have become very domineering in their leadership, and others who have refused to recognize the validity of the church membership of other Christians, and have excluded them from their meetings. I can recall being asked for a letter of introduction when, as a student in the 1970s, I attended a Brethren Assembly in Aberdeen! The apostle Paul complained about that very phenomenon in one of his epistles to the Corinthians: 'Do we need, like some people, letters of recommendation to you or from you? You yourselves are our letter, written on our hearts, known and read by everybody' (2 Cor. 3:1–2).

So we can see that the issues which Peter sought to address in his first-century circular letter from Rome to Asia Minor have continued to be live, into the twenty-first. Lording it is still a problematic set of attitudes and actions with which Christian congregations, assemblies, dioceses, and denominations must continue to reckon.

The earliest use of the title *kyrios*, 'lord', in the Hellenistic world of the inter-testamental period was that of 'Lord and King', *kyrios basileus*, which is found frequently between 64 and 50 BCE. In 12 BCE the Emperor Augustus (reigned 31 BCE–14 CE) was called *theos kai kyrios*, 'God and Lord', in Egypt, where Candace, Queen of Upper Egypt, was styled 'Mistress and Queen' (*kyria basilissa*), and the title *kyrios* was also given to Herod the Great (reigned 40–4 BCE), Agrippa I (reigned 39–44 CE), and Agrippa II (reigned 50–100 CE). High officials, as well as rulers, could receive this title. The term was also applied to the gods, who were often popularly referred to as 'lords'. Augustus, and his successor Tiberius (reigned 14–37 CE), both rejected the eastern form of monarchy, and with it all that was bound up with the title *kyrios*. However, Caligula (reigned 37–41 CE) was attracted to the title, and Nero (reigned 54–68 CE) was described in an inscription as 'Lord of all the world', indicating the increased frequency of this usage. One of the oldest recorded instances is found in Acts 25:26, on the lips of the Roman governor of Judaea, Porcius Festus, in his explanation to King Agrippa of Paul's appeal to Caesar: 'Because he made his appeal to the Emperor, I decided to send him to Rome. But I have nothing definite to write to His Majesty about him.' Reference to lordship here is not necessarily an expression of devotion to Caesar as a deity, as use of the title *kyrios* in and of itself did not mean calling the emperor a god. However, as the cult of Caesar developed, the title 'Lord' counted as a term of divinity, and it was the religious claims entailed by that which caused difficulties for Christians, and led to persecution by a totalitarian state.[16]

In the Septuagint the word *kyrios* is used over 9,000 times, translating the Hebrew *adon*, 'lord', and refers to men on only 190 of those occasions. In the majority of cases it replaces the Hebrew proper name of God, Yahweh, the LORD. In the New Testament, it occurs 717 times, the majority of which are in Luke–Acts and the Pauline epistles, which is understandable, as both authors were writing for people in the Hellenistic world. In contrast, the Gospel of Mark, which many believe is closely associated with Peter, is more connected with the Jewish Christian tradition, and contains only eighteen references. Sometimes the word reflects a secular significance, of the lord over against his slaves, for example, or of the owner of land or employer of servants. Interestingly, Peter uses the term of a husband (1 Pet. 3:6) in relation to his wife, an issue to which we shall return in the next chapter. However, God is frequently called *kyrios* in the New Testament, especially in numerous quotations from the Septuagint, and God, as Creator, is acknowledged as Lord of all (Acts 17:24). Above all, Jesus Christ is proclaimed Lord, both before and after the resurrection. Jesus of Nazareth was recognized as a Jewish rabbi ('my lord') in Mark 9:5, and in other places it is used to imply recognition of Jesus as leader, and a willingness to obey him (Mt. 7:21; 21:29ff). Even after his death, the words of the earthly Jesus are accorded ultimate authority for the Christian community, so that Paul could appeal to the Lord's words in order finally to decide a question (1 Cor. 7:10; 12:25). But the vast majority of occurrences refer to Christ the exalted Lord, including the confessional cry, 'Jesus Christ is Lord.' The exalted Christ rules over all humankind (Rom. 14:9) and all other powers in the universe must bow before him, so that God the Father is worshipped (Eph. 1:20f; 1 Pet. 3:22). In Revelation, John speaks of Jesus as the King of kings and Lord of lords. In this way, for the New Testament writers, the Lord Jesus Christ stands over against the many gods and lords of the pagan world.[17]

The verb *kyrieuein*, meaning 'to be a lord', 'to act as a master', or 'to be authorized', occurs more than fifty times in the Septuagint, and seven times in the New Testament, six of which are in Paul's writings, and one in Luke. The rule of kings over their people is characterized by ambition because of their misuse of power for selfish ends (Lk. 22:25), and Paul uses the verb to describe relationships of power. But the disciples were not to seek to be the greatest, but rather to serve like Jesus himself (Lk. 22:26f). Because Christ has risen, death no longer reigns over him, in that it no longer has any power over him (Rom. 6:9). Now that Christ has demonstrated his lordship over death, Christians must no longer let themselves be dominated by other powers. Paul declares that he does not wish to lord it over believers, but to work with them to make them joyful (2 Cor. 1:24). Peter, however, uses the stronger compound verb *katakyreuein* in 1 Peter 5:2, a word which the Septuagint uses mostly to denote domination by foreigners. It occurs only four times in the New Testament, often expressing the characteristic leadership style of Gentile rulers who lorded it over their people. The prefix *kata-* has a negative force, and implies that worldly princes exercise their rule to their own advantage, and contrary to the interests and well-being of their subjects (Mt. 20:25). This is what Paul Achtemeier calls 'high-handed authoritarianism'.[18]

Pastoral care – not coercion

The alternative to this negative leadership style is now presented by Peter: that of leading by example (5:3b). This ideal is very common in Paul's letters (see, for example, 1 Thess. 1:6; 2:14), but is found outside the Pauline corpus only in this passage. Of course, the supreme example of exemplary leadership is Jesus himself, a fact to which Peter alludes in 1 Peter 2:21–23 and 4:1, following Mark's record of the dominical claim to having come to be a servant (Mk. 10:42). In this way, we see that Peter's emphasis is that 'Christian leaders are, like good shepherds, to exercise their authority for the good of those entrusted to their care, not for their own satisfaction or enrichment.'[19] In other words, believers are not the subjects of their leaders, as may pertain in the secular realm, but rather, it is the case that all Christians belong to God, and so ministers, pastors or priests must carry out their duties as servants of God, and not as lords of the congregations, arrogant towards fellow Christians and arbitrarily exercising power over them. Peter reminds us that God is against such attitudes and actions, but, in contrast, is gracious to the humble

(1 Pet. 5:5b). However, as we have noted in Paul's teaching to Timothy (2 Tim. 4:1ff), this does not mean that Christian leaders are slavishly to follow popular demands and desires. The boot is not to be on the proverbial other foot, in other words! Servant-leadership is still leadership, and for leadership to function there must be those who are willing to be led. That's why the writer to the Hebrews exhorts:

> Remember your leaders, who spoke the word of God to you. Consider the outcome of their way of life and imitate their faith . . . Have confidence in your leaders and submit to their authority, because they keep watch over you as those who must give an account. Obey them so that their work will be a joy, not a burden, for that would be of no advantage to you (13:7, 17).[20]

Yet leaders must not forget the solemn warning of James 3:1: 'Not many of you should presume to be teachers, my brothers and sisters, because you know that we who teach will be judged more strictly.' In the next chapter, we will explore further what should be appropriate patterns for the proper exercise of authority in the church by bona fide Christian leaders, male and female, who recognize that they are ultimately accountable to God for their ministry.

Summary

Let's summarize our discussion in this chapter:

- We've noted that Peter had shared with Mark his memories of the teaching on leadership received from Jesus as the one who had come, supremely, not to be served but to serve. They were writing 1 Peter from Rome to unpack the implications of that ideal for the elders of struggling Christian communities in the eastern Empire.
- We've recognized that there were other models of leadership in the culture of Asia Minor, into which Peter was writing his first letter, especially the Roman *paterfamilias* and the Jewish synagogue elder. We noted that none of these provided the

early church with the example which they were to follow, so that Paul's associate, Priscilla, could be considered a model leader (elder/overseer), who excelled at teaching and exercised a strategic influence on house churches, working together with her husband Aquila.

- There was a temptation to adopt the domineering style of leadership which was exercised by some authorities in the secular world, but Peter reminds Christians of their call to respect those in positions of proper authority in both state and church, and not to emulate those who abuse their position.

- High-handed authoritarianism is as much to be abhorred today as it was in New Testament times, as Christian leaders are called to care for, rather than to dominate, those in their charge.

5

Authoritarianism and Feminism

We have seen that the focus of 1 Peter 5:1–5 is the authors' concern to deal with the vexed question of how Christians should treat one another in the shared life of the early churches in Asia Minor. Ramsey Michaels notes, 'Peter therefore focuses on those whose responsibility it is to take the initiative in such relationships.'[1] The closest parallel to his exhortations to the elders in 1 Peter is Paul's speech to the Ephesian elders in Acts 20:17–38, where Paul sets himself up as an example to support his command to 'Keep watch over yourselves and all the flock of which the Holy Spirit has made you overseers. Be shepherds of the church of God' (Acts 20:28; cf. 1 Pet. 5:2–3). That was to continue his apostolic support for the house churches in and around the great city of Ephesus, capital of the province of Asia, and home of the huge temple of the goddess Artemis, which was much larger than the Parthenon in Athens. We noted that Paul had left Priscilla and Aquila in charge of the work in Ephesus (Acts 18:19). He went home to mission base at Antioch in Syria, but returned to Ephesus not long afterwards, via the overland route through Asia Minor. There followed a very fruitful time of mission and ministry for Paul in Ephesus, which Luke describes, as an eyewitness, in Acts 19:1 – 20:1. Events included considerable adverse reaction to Paul's preaching, notably from those who profited from the manufacture and sale of idols of Artemis, and a riot broke out. The crowd was whipped up into a fury, shouting again and again, 'Great is Artemis of the Ephesians!' (19:28, 34). The city clerk then intervened and spoke to calm the crowd with these words:

People of Ephesus, doesn't all the world know that the city of Ephesus is the guardian of the temple of the great Artemis and of her image, which fell from heaven? Therefore, since these facts are undeniable, you ought to calm down and not do anything rash. You have brought these men here, though they have neither robbed temples nor blasphemed our goddess (19:35–7).

After saying this, he dismissed the crowd, and when the uproar was ended, Paul sent for the disciples, encouraged them, and then set sail for Macedonia.

Paul travelled through Greece and then sailed to the eastern Mediterranean, stopping briefly at Miletus, near to Ephesus, en route. There he met with the elders/overseers of the Ephesian church, and reminded them of the hard but fruitful ministry they had shared together. He said that he felt compelled by the Holy Spirit to go back to Jerusalem, convicted that prison and suffering awaited him there. He was convinced that none of those leaders would ever see him again. But he was not ashamed of his gospel service among them, 'For I have not hesitated to proclaim to you the whole will of God. Keep watch over yourselves and all the flock of which the Holy Spirit has made you overseers . . .' (Acts 20:27–28).

Peter's feminism

The significant fact to note, for our discussion, is that Priscilla and Aquila might have been among those who knelt with Paul to pray on that beach near Ephesus as he prepared to face the toughest ordeal of his life, had they not returned to Rome from Ephesus some time before Paul wrote Romans. We know that the apostle was writing his great epistle from Corinth on his third missionary journey, about 57 CE, and he lists Aquila and Priscilla first in his greetings to the Roman church at the start of Romans 16. As we have noted, Priscilla was one of the Ephesian elders/overseers who had engaged in a joint teaching ministry with her husband, and Priscilla was a woman! That was a radical departure from patterns of male-only leadership which were typical of the cultures of Roman Asia Minor. Ramsey Michael's suggestion, that there is a close parallel between Peter's paraenesis to the elders of the churches in Asia Minor and Paul's famous meeting with the Ephesian church leaders, is seminal, because Peter has important things to say in his first letter regarding the role of women in church and society. We cannot attempt to apply Peter's insights about authoritarianism to our contemporary church situation, until we have sought to understand his radical feminism in comparison with the social expectations of his day.[2]

We are introduced to this possibility in Luke's presentation of Peter's speeches and postures in Acts. After the Ascension the group of disciples, including Peter, met in Jerusalem, and they joined in prayer 'along with the women and Mary the mother of Jesus' (Acts 1:13–14). Prior to Pentecost it is true that they drew lots to find a male replacement for Judas Iscariot, but at Pentecost Peter speaks emphatically of its meaning: 'This is what was spoken by the prophet Joel . . . your sons **and** daughters will prophesy . . . Even on my servants **both men and women** I will pour out my Spirit in those days and they will prophesy' (2:16–18). Again, Peter prays in 4:29, '"Enable your servants to speak your word with great boldness" . . . They were all filled with the Holy Spirit and spoke the word of God boldly' (using generic terms to include male and female). In Acts 10:34 Peter confesses, 'I now realise how true it is that God does not show favouritism but accepts those from every nation who fear him and do what is right.' Like Paul, Peter was committed to establishing leadership patterns which broke the mould and truly proclaimed liberation for women and men. To revert to Roman or Jewish styles of male-only leadership, which would have been comfortable culturally, was not their intention.

But this raises important questions which have disturbed many Christian leaders ever since, because we have to address the controversial issue of feminism against the background of the historical interpretation of the New Testament, which has consistently expressed the view that the apostles Paul and Peter, as Jewish Christians of their age, must have adopted the gender bias which they had learned in Judaism, where no woman could be a rabbi, in any synagogue. Rabbi literally means 'My lord', and assumptions have clearly been made that automatically connect church leadership with family headship. The argument goes that if Peter and

Paul taught that married women were subject to their husbands' lordship, in some sense, and Paul specifically forbade women from contributing teaching when the Corinthian church gathered (1 Cor. 14:33b–35), then they would never have appointed a woman elder (priest, pastor, minister) in any of the churches which they established. But is this either exegetically sound, or ethically safe?

Before we turn to Peter's paraenesis about the role of women in 1 Peter, we must review this issue with the help of Richard Bauckham's recent study, from which we have already cited above. He is particularly interested in the role of women as witnesses of the resurrection in the Gospels, and seeks to place such claims against the cultural and social background of Palestinian Judaism and the Greco–Roman world. For example, he notes that, in general, women were not considered eligible to be witnesses in Jewish courts.[3] Josephus provides the reasoning for this as 'the levity and impetuosity of their sex'.[4] However, Josephus does not always rule out the possibility of God speaking directly to or through a woman, in the scriptures of the Septuagint, with which he was familiar, yet he seems to minimize such occurrences.[5] Bauckham also states that in the Greco–Roman world of the first century CE there is considerable evidence that educated men often thought of women as gullible in matters of religion.[6] He cites the example of the philosopher Strabo who asserted: 'In dealing with a crowd of women . . . a philosopher cannot influence them by reason or exhort them to reverence, piety and faith.'[7]

In contrast to this, we find a very different picture in the Gospel resurrection stories, where women are presented as being given priority by God as recipients of revelation and therefore as 'mediators of that revelation to men'.[8] Bauckham sees this as part and parcel of the great reversal implied in Christian eschatology, in which God promises that the first will be last and the last first.[9] He enquires why Matthew's Gospel, with its strong depiction of Peter as the rock upon whose witness the church will be established, should attribute the first resurrection appearance to the women of the apostolic circle, and make no reference to the appearance to Peter which is mentioned both by Luke and Paul.[10] In addition, Mary's testimony in John 20:18, 'I have seen the

Lord', should be compared with what the other disciples later said to Thomas: 'We have seen the Lord!' (20:25). Her claim to be an authentic witness of the risen Christ is surely to be placed alongside that of the apostle Paul, in 1 Corinthians 9:1: 'Am I not an apostle? Have I not seen Jesus our Lord?' This clearly demonstrates, says Bauckham, that the role of women as witnesses of the resurrection was highly regarded in the early Christian communities.[11]

It is also significant, in terms of Bauckham's argument, that the problematic ending of Mark's Gospel plays its part in the quest to appreciate the role of women in the early church. Most scholars agree that Mark should finish with 16:8, 'Trembling and bewildered, the women went out and fled from the tomb. They said nothing to anyone, because they were afraid.' However, the women's silence here is not due to a fear of speaking out, but rather because, in their society and culture, men are considered to be the legitimate speakers in the public arena.[12] This is underlined in Mark's passion narrative, where we see the male disciples failing in their duty, and two important anecdotes involving women. The first is that of the anointing of Jesus at Bethany (14:3–9), and the second is the visit of the women to the tomb (16:1–8). The woman who anoints Jesus is depicted as the first person, male or female, who accepts that Jesus has to die. The women at the tomb are the first people to know that Christ is risen.[13]

We shall bear these insights in mind as we explore in some detail the teaching of 1 Peter on the role of women in Christian leadership. Michaels notes that Peter's use of *presbyteroi* in 1 Peter 5:5 is a generic use of the word, and need not imply that elders were always male: 'Since Peter seems to have little exact knowledge of the forms of ministry in the congregations to which he is writing, he probably intends to leave open the gender of the "elders" as well, both here and in v 1.'[14] So it was not impossible for Peter to imagine female elders 'lording it' over male members of the congregations, as well as for overbearing male elders to be dominating female disciples. Elders were to learn appropriate servant-leadership styles, and those who were led, whom Peter generically categorizes as *neoteroi*, 'younger ones' (5:5), were to defer to the proper authority of the elders. The style of this is similar to the household duty code which

Peter adopts in 3:1–7, and we must spend some time expounding those verses:

> You wives too must defer to your husbands, so that any among them who are disobedient to the word might be won over by their wives' conduct. Your gentleness should not consist of externals, such as your braided hair and the gold you put on, or the clothes you wear. It is rather the person hidden in your heart, with that imperishable quality of a humble and quiet spirit. It is (an adornment) most lavish in God's sight. That was how the holy wives who hoped in God adorned themselves long ago, by deferring to their husbands. Sarah, for example, obeyed Abraham when she called him 'Lord'. You have become her children; so do good and let nothing frighten you. You husbands too must know how to live with a woman, showing respect as somebody weaker – even as co–heirs of the grace of life. That way your prayers will not be hindered.[15]

Women and men – joint heirs

Here, Peter focuses on the interests of women, as potentially oppressed partners in marriage, in line with his purpose in this letter, and outlines the mutual obligations of husbands and wives. It fits in well with what Peter has already dealt with, as he has outlined his views on household duties, from 2:13 on, beginning with advice to domestic slaves. The advice to married women is in three parts: first of all an exhortation to defer to the husband's proper authority, secondly an admonition about what pleases God, and thirdly an illustration of appropriate attitudes, from the example of Sarah and Abraham in the Old Testament. Submission, or deference in certain social relationships, is defined by Peter as 'doing good' or doing what God requires, despite opposition or danger. Here, proper wifely deference is connected with modesty in dress and make-up, just as in Paul's parallel passage in 1 Timothy 2:9–10: 'I also want women to dress modestly, with decency and propriety, not with elaborate hair-styles or gold or pearls or expensive clothes, but with good deeds, appropriate for women who profess to worship God.'[16]

Because 1 Peter 3:1–6 is clearly addressing some wealthy women, among others, this reference to Sarah is particularly well-focused. Although she was a wife of a *paroikos*, and they were resident aliens for much of their life together as pastoral nomads, it is recorded at the beginning of the story of Abraham's journey from Mesopotamia to Canaan, in Genesis 12:5, that they had considerable possessions and many servants. This insight should be placed alongside our earlier discussion about the social status of the majority of Christians, as resident aliens in Asia Minor, at the time 1 Peter was written. In modern times, that phenomenon has been reflected in the comparative wealth of many Jewish families of the diaspora, which has often been used as an excuse for anti-semitism. In the same way, marginalized Christians in first-century Asia Minor may not all have been poor, but rather hard-working and successful business people, like Lydia from Thyatira in the province of Asia, the salesperson of purple cloth, whom Paul met when he preached in Macedonia (Acts 16:11–15).

The appeal of Peter, therefore, has two main points, which may have been related to that kind of female financial success, or marriage to wealthy husbands.[17] First of all, the women were reminded of the precedent of 'holy wives who hoped in God', in v. 5, and this is linked with the prior reference to clothes and make-up. Secondly, Peter affirmed that 'You have become Sarah's daughters', in v. 6, by their proper deference to their husbands as 'lord', which means continuing to do good and not being fearful. Our present concern is to understand what Peter means when he commends Sarah for calling Abraham 'lord', or 'master' (NIV).

Peter says that 'Sarah obeyed Abraham, and called him her "Lord"' (v. 6). This is his concrete example of proper deference to husbands by wives who are committed Christians. The reference is to Genesis 18:12 in the Septuagint, where Sarah, on hearing God's promise of a son in her old age, laughed and said, 'This has never yet happened to me, and my lord is too old!' Peter does not reflect on the doubt and amusement which Sarah expressed (18:13–15), but focuses on her use of *kyrios* (Hebrew *adon*). Unlike some of the husbands of whom Peter is speaking, Abraham was clearly a believer who was not opposing Sarah's faith in any way. The use of *kyrios* is confusing in a Christian context, of course, because of the confession 'Jesus Christ is Lord', which every believer would have made at baptism. Christian wives knew where their ultimate allegiance lay. Peter normally uses the verb *hypotassesthai*, 'to defer to', in outlining household duties, rather than *hypakouein*, 'to obey', which he uses only once in the letter, in 3:6. His uses of the cognate *hypakoē*, 'obedience' (1:2, 14, 22) do not refer to social relationships, but to Christian conversion or faith. At any rate, the context of Sarah's 'obedience' is not quiet submissiveness, but rather of bemused scepticism at the extravagant promise of a child at her advanced age.

The solution, suggests Michaels, is not to get too bogged down in the minutiae of interpreting this verse, and rather to recognize that Peter focuses on one word, *kyrios*:

> His point is not that Christian wives 'revere . . . the Lord Christ' (3:15) by obeying their husbands, as if the husband played the role of Christ to the wife; the phrase 'as to the Lord' in Ephesians 5:22 should not be read into 1 Peter . . . His attention is therefore focused on Sarah and her behaviour, not on who Abraham was or how he treated her. His argument is from the greater to the lesser: if Sarah 'obeyed' Abraham and called him 'Lord', the Christian wives in Asia should at least treat their husbands with deference and respect.[18]

Peter could have reinforced his point by adopting the tactics of some interpreters, in certain Hellenistic Jewish circles at the time, which made a meal of Sarah's supposed significance, often adopting allegorical methods. 'He does not want Christian wives to assume the spiritual responsibility of leading their pagan husbands out of darkness into light, only to be good wives, and not to be discouraged or intimidated by their husband's unbelief. God will take care of the rest.'[19] This reflects what Peter has already said, in 3:1, about proper submission to husbands, 'so that, if any of them do not believe the word, they may be won over without words'. The punchline is, rather, 'You are her daughters if you do what is right, then, and do not give way to fear' (3:6b). 'Do what is right' defines what Peter means by 'defer', but not in the sense that a wife's moral responsibility is defined by her submission to her husband. For example, a Christian wife's deference should not include adopting his religion, as this would be the very opposite of doing good and obeying the Lord's will. In fact, as the result of her faithfulness to God, a Christian wife might suffer abuse at the hands of a persecuting pagan husband. It is certain that, within those first-century cultures of the eastern Empire, wives were expected to assume the religion of their husbands, because the household expressed its solidarity in a common religion, and refusal to share in that solidarity was perceived to be a threat both to the family and to the state.[20] If Peter encouraged wives not to fear any terror, he must have been aware of examples of the very real pressure under which many Christian women lived. Moreover, he must have known the ancient Proverbs, which he seems to cite in 1 Peter: 'Hatred stirs up dissension, but love covers over all wrongs' (Prov. 10:12; cf. 4:8), and 'If the righteous receive their due on earth, how much more the ungodly and the sinner!' (Prov. 11:31; cf. 4:17). In 5:5, he also cites Proverbs 3:34, 'He mocks proud mockers, but shows favour to the humble and oppressed.' So it is likely that the source of Peter's advice to wives who may fear possible abuse, is, in fact, Proverbs 3:25–26: 'Have no fear of sudden disaster or of the ruin that overtakes the wicked, for the LORD will be at your side and will keep your foot from being snared.' In this way, Peter touches on a theme which is only too familiar to the modern reader in the Western world of the twenty-first century, where domestic abuse is a very real fear for many women, as illustrated in the recent film *Sleeping with the Enemy*, starring Julia Roberts.[21]

That brings us to the last verse in this key text, 1 Peter 3:7:

> Husbands, in the same way be considerate as you live with your wives, and treat them with respect as the weaker partner and as heirs with you of the gracious gift of life, so that nothing will hinder your prayers.

This exhortation begins by connecting with Peter's paraenesis on appropriate civil, household, and ecclesiastical conduct, which is rooted in the original command in 2:17, 'Show proper respect to everyone.' Achtemeier notes that the Greek words chosen by the writer here indicate that this exhortation is not addressed to husbands only, but has a wider meaning, probably referring to the way males in a household deal with its female members.[22] Men are

reminded here of a woman's comparative physical frailty and
socio-cultural disadvantage, in their situations in Asia Minor at the
time, rather than applying any concept of inherent universal spiritual or moral weakness to the female of the species. All human
beings are God's creatures, and there can, therefore, be no justification for any, male or female, to take advantage of another's perceived weaker position. Christian women and men are co-heirs of
the grace of life, says Peter, which gives further reason for men not
to adopt the normal cultural attitude towards women, which was
current, as they are all equal before God. It is his version of Paul's
affirmation in Galatians 3:28, which was delivered to churches in
south-central Asia Minor, at least fifteen years before 1 Peter was
written and distributed: 'There is neither Jew nor Gentile, neither
slave nor free, neither male nor female, for you are all one in Christ
Jesus.' The weight which is behind the apostolic affirmation, in this
culturally controversial area of their teaching and exhortation, is
further seen in Peter's eschatological emphasis. 'The gracious gift
of life' means 'Grace that consists in life', and refers to the new life
which believers have inherited in Christ, of which they have
already received a foretaste, while there is much more yet to come,
following God's judgment of the world at the end of the age.

No cultural compromise

There is also a very practical reason for men to show real respect
to their womenfolk, for lack of such treatment will affect the effi-
cacy of their prayers to God, who will simply not listen to them.
It seems that Peter is focusing particularly on the men's prayers,
and threatening them with spiritual disaster if they adopt a domineering manner with their wives and other women in their
households. Otherwise it would seem very strange that women
are to be penalized in prayer through the disobedience of men.
Achtemeier therefore notes, 'The point is clear: men who transfer
cultural notions about the superiority of men over women into
the Christian community lose their ability to communicate with
God.'[23]

So we see how 1 Peter is clearly a broadside against Christian
compromise with cultures which are not informed by biblical

values and the message of life in Christ, which is the gospel. Such advice about women and men was not typical of other contemporary household codes. 1 Peter 3:7 is included to warn men in general, and husbands in particular, that the teaching on female submission by Christian wives to pagan husbands, in 3:1–6, does not imply that male members of the Christian community can dominate the womenfolk in the manner typical in secular society at the time. There can be no justification, in other words, for any belief in female inferiority. There is an essential equality between women and men in the Christian community, and they are 'together and equally heirs of God's grace that promises life in the age to come'.[24]

However, some of my readers, both Catholic and evangelical, may have been very uneasy about my developing argument, in chapters 2 – 4, when it has included a claim that Peter advocated radical feminism in terms of his own understanding of how to live the Christian life, and engage in Christian community, in societies which were, as yet, relatively untouched by the culturally transformational message of the gospel. They will immediately think of the apostle Paul's teaching in 1 Corinthians and 1 Timothy, in which he apparently argues for a quite different approach, exegetically and ethically. Before we move on to the next chapter, those who are concerned about this issue should read the extended endnote.[25] In the meantime, we do have, briefly, to address the meaning of male headship in Paul's theology, in so far as that may impinge on our discussion of church leadership.

Colin Brown has provided us with an excellent review of the vexed question of Paul's understanding of male headship, in relation to Christian worship.[26] He notes that 1 Corinthians 11:2–15 contains a discussion of why women should be 'covered' when they attend public worship, meaning either the wearing of a veil, or long hair. For Paul, suggests Brown, the role and relationships of the sexes, which are determined by the order of creation, are not abolished by salvation. Paul's argument is based on two points: first, that it is appropriate to cover one's head in the presence of a superior, and secondly, the constitutional relationship of man and woman, which gives a certain priority to man. Given those premises, for Paul, the 'covering' of women in worship logically follows.

It is a matter of recognized hierarchical order, in other words. Brown concludes, 'However, in a situation where the former premise is neither recognized nor understood, the validity of the conclusion no longer has the same weight as it did in Paul's day.'[27] Brown also comments on Paul's use of arguments about the priority of man over women in the order of creation, in relation to the glory of God, and concludes that the practical application which might be drawn from this depends on how far they are understood and recognized in a community.[28] Even more obscure, to twenty-first-century readers, is Paul's appeal to the angels (1 Cor. 11:10), as a reason for a woman's head being covered in worship. Again, Brown concludes that in a culture where the significance of veiling or wearing long hair is no longer understood in the same way, the argument no longer has the same force.

This is an important conclusion for our developing understanding of leadership roles in the church, too, because F.F. Bruce states that Paul's implication is that every believer should understand that head, in this sense, does not mean 'ruler' or 'chief', but 'source' or 'origin'.[29] The creation narrative of Genesis 2:21ff assigns a certain priority to man. But the Christian knows that Christ has a greater priority, as the archetypal man, and the head of Christ is God. As Paul says in 1 Corinthians 11:3: 'The head of every man is Christ, and the head of the woman is man, and the head of Christ is God', but there is no agreement among scholars as to whether recognition of this headship is ultimately about authority or respect or both.

Peter's circular letter

We should follow Brown's humility, then, and not allow the disputed understanding of headship to be integral to our current discussion. There may well have been opaque cultural issues at stake in Corinth which concerned matters of appropriate female behaviour in worship and which were specific to the situation in Achaia which Paul was addressing. Unlike the Corinthian correspondence, which was sent to a group of house churches in a major Greek city, 1 Peter was a circular letter which contained much more generally applicable teaching and exhortation, and, so the present author believes, is therefore more significant in our quest for a balanced practical theology of Christian leadership styles, now as then. At any rate, Christian leadership was always corporate, and never monarchical. Peter speaks here to the elders, plural, who worked together to oversee the mission and ministry of the churches of Asia Minor. Out of that evolved the need for team leaders, or bishops, who were effectively captains of the growing regional groups of overseers of house churches. That was surely good sense, from a human resources management point of view. It is fairly easy to understand why, by the time the aged apostle John, the Elder, sent his three Epistles and the Revelation to the churches of Asia, about twenty-five years after 1 Peter was written, he seems to have a stronger self–awareness of his episcopal authority than Peter had from Rome to his distant charges in Asia Minor. Yet he was still 'the Elder', as Peter had styled himself, in his rhetorical device to win the hearts and minds of his hearers.

The twenty-first-century Western churches surely need to recover that sense of team leadership. In Africa today, south of the Sahara, it goes without saying that most of the ongoing church leadership is effected by groups of part–time, tentmaker elders, who evangelize, teach, and exercise pastoral care, and only occasionally benefit from the immediate ministry of a pastor, minister, or priest. I warmly remember the Revd Robert Wafula, a minister of the Christian Reformed Church in Kenya, whom I met when he was undergoing postgraduate work in Edinburgh. He told me of his life and work as a Bible translator during the week and as a pastor at the weekend, and how he was married to a hospital chaplain who had just given birth to a son, whom they named Grace! He was responsible for a number of parishes, and visited them each on a rota, every six weeks or so. Each weekend, he would take his bike to the bus and travel for many miles, before disembarking and cycling quite a distance to the location of his church for that week. Then he would reverse the journey after he had taken services, with the sacraments, on Sunday. His story left me breathless, especially when I realized that Robert was very lame in one leg! In that part of Africa, the heretical division between 'clergy' and 'laity' is practically unrecognized in many denominations, because of the reality of meeting the needs of expanding churches. And yet in Scotland, the motherland of Presbyterianism, so many professing Christian people are content to follow Ignatius's ancient appeal, 'Do nothing without the bishop (minister, priest, pastor)', and literally do virtually nothing as a result! Is it any wonder, then, that we are experiencing church shrink?

But, before we begin to gather the many threads of our discussion together and begin to apply Peter's paraenesis to our contemporary culture and church situation, there is another dimension, which we cannot ignore. In the section following our key text, 1 Peter 5:1–5, the writer goes on to say this:

> Be alert and of sober mind. Your enemy the devil prowls around like a roaring lion looking for someone to devour. Resist him, standing firm in the faith (5:8–9).

In the next chapter, our focus will be principalities and powers.

Summary

Let's summarize what we have learned in this chapter:

- We've come to realize that Peter's project includes his personal advocacy of a radical feminism, in comparison with typical expectations and attitudes in the cultures and religious communities of his day within the eastern Roman Empire, to which he wrote 1 Peter.
- We've noticed that one of the problems faced by Christian women at the time was being married to unbelieving husbands in a culture which expected wives to convert to their spouse's religion. Despite that, Peter exhorts women to carry on seeking to do God's will, and to respect the proper authority of their husbands. Christian women and men are joint heirs of God's gracious gift of eternal life in Christ.
- 1 Peter undermines Christian compromise with cultures which sustain oppressive regimes and the abuse of women and of others who may be perceived as socially or physically weaker than naturally dominant men.

- Peter's teaching on church leadership is of more general application than much of Paul's, as Peter was writing circular letters rather than those which were specifically geared to deal with particular problems in named city fellowships.

6

Authorities and Powers

With the decline in influence of theological liberalism in the Western churches, there has come a renewed interest in the supernatural. This was partly the result of the charismatic movement, which influenced the mainline Christian denominations from the 1960s and into the new millennium. Among many scholars, this rehabilitation was due to the seminal trilogy of Walter Wink, *The Powers* (1984–92),[1] which gave a radical slant on ancient questions concerning the existence of evil. Around that time, at a more popular level, the influential psychiatrist and writer M. Scott Peck raised broader awareness of such issues in a bestselling book, *People of the Lie: the Hope for Healing Human Evil*. For many preachers, exposition of Paul's teaching on spiritual warfare in Ephesians 6:10–18 has been an essential strategy in rearming the churches for spiritual struggle. However, the emphasis of Peter in his two extant epistles has not been given the attention it deserves, largely due to continued controversy over certain aspects of interpretation, the vexed question of the authorship of 1 Peter, and historical tensions between Roman Catholic and Reformed traditions regarding the priority or supremacy of Peter among the apostles. I accept the apostolic authorship and reject as spurious the alleged pseudonymity of the letter as a view which is based on assumptions that are open to question and is not, as some still maintain, 'an assured result of modern scholarship'. In fact, the overwhelming evidence from key early Christian sources is the recognition that this letter came from Peter's apostolic circle, and that it was in circulation well before the end of the first century. The elevated Greek style of 1 Peter can be explained by the fact that it was quite normal for letters to be composed by an amanuensis, who could have been given freedom in the choice of language, to communicate the basic ideas of an author. Remember that Mark and Silas are mentioned in the text as being involved with the writing and transmission of 1 Peter, which indicates that we would be wrong to imagine that apostolic letters were always the sole work of the apostles, any more than are all speeches delivered by the President of the US today his sole work. In fact, Peter's incarceration in Rome prior to his martyrdom may well have meant that he needed to use speech writers! Yet that does nothing to diminish the apostolic authority with which 1 Peter is invested.

We have noted that the literary style of this epistle, paraenesis, is a form of ethical exhortation which has as its aim the persuasion and motivation of Peter's hearers in Asia Minor. In a similar way, Luke and Timothy were probably key aides to Paul in the writing of at least some of his letters, and other associates may well have been involved at other times, too. The point of this is to focus our attention on the fact that the early Christian leaders engaged in corporate strategic decision-making, as we see from Luke's accounts, in Acts 13:1–3, of the developing mission base at Antioch in Syria, where there were prophets and teachers (elders) along with Barnabas and Paul, and in Acts 15:1–29, of the Jerusalem Council, where apostles and elders, together with the whole church, were involved in the decision-making process. The apostles did not act as 'little Caesars' over their supposed allotted domains, as some imagine, despite the later development of the benevolent patriarchal leadership model, which Aleksandr Solzhenitsyn has described as Caesaro-papism.[2] There was also a degree of interdependence between apostles like Paul and Peter, as clearly stated by the latter, a phenomenon which is also seen in connections between Peter's epistles and the letter of James, as we shall see. Because of this, we have to interpret the New Testament canonically, and accept the fact that the early church recognized the supreme authority of the documents that we now call the New Testament, and included them among 'the scriptures', largely because of their origin in the four principal apostolic mission circles of James/Matthew (including Jude?), Peter/Mark (including Jude?), Paul/Luke (including Hebrews), and John. Geographically, their respective mission bases were

Jerusalem, Caesarea/Rome, Antioch, and Southern Palestine/ Ephesus.[3] We need look no further for the origin of the idea of the canon, or authoritative apostolic writings, than Peter's words, 'Our dear brother Paul wrote to you with the wisdom that God gave him . . . His letters contain some things that are hard to understand, which ignorant and unstable people distort, as they do the other Scriptures' (2 Pet. 3:15–16).[4]

Evil – personal, social, ecclesiastical

Peter believed that he was struggling against spiritual opposition, as did Paul, and that he needed to prepare his people to engage in spiritual warfare. As the composition of the apostolic message, which was to be the vehicle for the 'sword of the Spirit, which is the word of God' (Eph. 6:17), was a strategic matter for each apostolic group, so was the dissemination and demonstration of the truths of the scriptures we now call the New Testament. The early Christians thought of themselves not only as a family, but as a family at war, and they believed themselves to be fighting, ultimately, not against human beings, but against organized spiritual opposition. We're familiar with Paul's teaching on authorities and powers in Ephesians 6 (also in Eph. 1:21; 3:10; Rom. 8:38; 1 Thess. 5:8), but let's not forget that similar insights are found in 1 and 2 Peter. For Peter, awareness of such struggles was rooted in his experience of suffering for Christ, which was common among his hearers in Asia Minor. In 1 Peter 1:6-7, he speaks of their joyful faith, yet reminds them that 'Now for a little while you may have had to suffer grief in all kinds of trials . . . so that your faith . . . may be proved genuine . . .' Yet he also exposes the awful reality that, far from being proved genuine, Christians might use their freedom as a cover-up for evil (2:16), and so refuse to bear unjust suffering as an essential part of their witness (2:19–20). Christians, as par for the course, from time to time will have to suffer for doing good (2:20–21). In fact, this is part of the calling of Christ, who first suffered for his people. It is part of what it means to follow Jesus (2:21–25). In suffering for the flock, Jesus demonstrated his love, as 'Shepherd and Overseer of your souls' (2:25). In this way, we see that Christian leaders were particularly warned to expect unjust suffering as a normal part of their service. As Peck notes, 'Great leaders, when wise and well, are likely to endure degrees of anguish unknown to the common man.'[5] If the Chief Shepherd had been ill-treated by his opponents, then the under-shepherds would receive similar treatment.

Peter goes on to specify the loci of that kind of suffering, for ministers and ordinary members of the churches. There will, first of all, be tensions with the civil authorities and employers of servants and slaves (2:13–19). Secondly, there will be tensions in the home, between unbelieving husbands and Christian wives, in particular (3:1–7). But there will also, thirdly, be tensions within the churches themselves (3:8–12), so that believers will have to learn to overcome their differences and to live in harmony with one another: to be sympathetic, loving, compassionate and humble. Instead of giving as good as they get, Christians should not repay evil with evil, but with good, as they pursue the way of peace together. Fourthly, there will be both opportunities and threats in relation to their pagan neighbours (3:13–17). At times they will struggle with very real fears as they suffer for doing good, but this should not put them off being ready to give a reason for their Christian hope, as opportunity arises, even if they are sometimes being misunderstood, and are often the focus of destructive gossip. That brings us to Peter's punchline, and the fifth area where Christians will experience struggle: 'It is better, if it is God's will, to suffer for doing good than for doing evil. For Christ also suffered once for sins . . . but made alive in the Spirit. In that state he went and made proclamation to the imprisoned spirits . . . baptism saves you . . . by the resurrection of Jesus Christ, who has gone into heaven and is at God's right hand – with angels, authorities and powers in submission to him' (3:17–22).

Much ink has been spilled about the meaning of this passage, but, as usual, it becomes clearer when we examine the context and the section as a whole. Peter is speaking about spiritual warfare. He is saying that Jesus Christ has definitively defeated evil spirits through his death and resurrection, and that his victory has been demonstrated to the spirit world.[6] Paul has the same notion, in Colossians 2:15: 'Having disarmed the powers and authorities, he made a public spectacle of them, triumphing over them by the cross.' Yet, despite the fact that the enemy has been disabled, both Peter and Paul warn believers that the war is not over. Oscar Cullmann famously likened our spiritual situation between the two comings of Christ to that which pertained after D-Day in World War II.[7] The Nazis were defeated, in principle, when the Allies established beachheads in France, yet there would be another year of bloody war in Europe before they surrendered. Realizing that they were fighting a losing battle, they determined to make things as difficult as possible for the Allies, as they had much to lose. The apostles, as pioneer mission commanders, were completely realistic about the nature of the struggles into which they were leading their Christian soldiers. Like Churchill in wartime, they could only promise, in the interim, 'blood, toil, sweat, and tears'. Christian experience is not genuine, or at least lacks credibility, if it acknowledges nothing of that demonic dimension. From the beginning, their Lord had taught Peter and the other disciples to pray, 'Deliver us from evil.' He had also modelled that in the Garden of Gethsemane, when he challenged the disciples to 'Watch and pray so that you will not fall into temptation' (Mk. 14:38), while he himself struggled spiritually in prayer.

Spiritual warfare

Yet the apostles could also declare the good news that, ultimately, the church of Christ is on the winning side. Jesus Christ, says Peter, is at God's right hand, with angels, authorities and powers in submission to him (1 Pet. 3:22). That means that he has returned to his position as the eternal Image of God, for whom and through whom all things were made, and in whom all things hold together (Col. 1:15–17). In this way, when faced by the reality of spiritual struggle, Christians can be assured that God has supplied the churches with tactical defensive and offensive measures. Peter says that it is possible for believers to 'Arm yourselves' (1 Pet. 4:1). There follows an outline of the equipment required by Christian soldiers who want to take their stand against the enemy. In Ephesians 6:10ff, Paul's famous teaching on the full armour of God begins with an exhortation to be strong in the Lord in order to take one's stand against the devil and his schemes. In 1 Peter the starting point is to focus on the attitude of Christ himself, as Paul does in Philippians 2:1–11, and then to exhort Christians not to live out their lives according to evil human desires, but rather to do the will of God. At the same time, they are to look back and remember the pagan lifestyle from which Christ has delivered them, and in which they had 'spent enough time' in 'debauchery, lust, drunkenness, orgies, carousing, and detestable idolatry' (4:3). They should not fall into the temptation to go back to their evil ways, despite pressures from their pagan neighbours to do so (4:4). At the same time, like Christ they should be clear-minded and self-controlled so that they can pray, and not be overwhelmed by temptation (4:7). Peter concludes:

> Above all, love each other deeply, because love covers over a multitude of sins. Offer hospitality to one another without grumbling. Each one should use whatever gift he has received to serve others, as faithful stewards of God's grace in its various forms. If you speak, you should do so as one who speaks the very words of God. If you serve, you should do so with the strength God provides . . . To him be the glory and power . . . Amen (4:8–11).

In this way, Peter shows how active Christian living and leadership is the only antidote to the negative attitudes and actions which could so easily infiltrate the churches and injure fellowship. He simplifies the main spiritual giftings under the headings of 'speaking' and 'serving' (which probably corresponds to Paul's distinction between elders/overseers and deacons). The former is of chief concern to our discussion here. In Peter's mind, proper motivation for the ministry of the word is a very important factor. Elders/overseers are to teach as those 'bringing words from God' as they exercise their ministry in the context of Christian worship. They must realize the responsibility which is theirs, in other words, not to pontificate, but rather to pass on that which has been revealed by God through the apostle-prophets, because they will be judged by that, in the long term. Peter then summarizes the nature of the Christian struggle, and reminds us that the intensity of this should be no surprise, in view of what he has said. In fact, it is a cause for real joy, as their suffering is a sign that they are really living in fellowship with Christ, who suffered for them. 'If you suffer,' says Peter, 'it should not be as a murderer or thief or any other kind of criminal, or even as a meddler. However, if you suffer as a Christian, do not be ashamed, but praise God that you bear that name. For it is time for judgment to begin with God's household; and if it begins with us, what will be the outcome for those who do not obey the gospel of God? . . . So, then, those who suffer according to God's will should commit themselves to their faithful Creator and continue to do good' (4:15–19).

Through prayer and a Christ-like attitude, therefore, realistic Christians can learn to overcome evil in their individual lives and in the corporate life of the church, as well as in their daily interaction with unbelievers in the real world. Peter's paraenesis pulls no punches. His ethical exhortation speaks about real struggles which typify the daily lives of his hearers and himself. Yet he is saying that behind the scenes there is another battle going on, in the spiritual realm. Inhabiting the structures of family, church, and society, as well as invading personal individual experience, there are other authorities and powers at work.

And that leads us into our key text, 1 Peter 5:1–5, and what follows in 5:8–9, concerning the work of the devil: 'Be alert and of sober mind. Your enemy the devil prowls around like a roaring lion looking for someone to devour. Resist him, standing firm in the faith, because you know that your fellow believers throughout the world are undergoing the same kind of sufferings.' In other words, Peter's warnings and advice about the powers of evil, and how to handle them, are integral to his entire message in this letter about the place of suffering in the Christian life, and the standard struggles, which all believers must learn to survive.

At the same time, let us not forget that Peter was acutely aware of the insidious influence of evil, even within the first group of disciples. He was, according to his memoir contained in Mark 8:29, the first publicly to confess his belief that Jesus of Nazareth was the Messiah. Yet when Christ then began openly to teach them that he had to suffer many things, be killed and rise from death on the third day, Peter took him aside and rebuked him.

Jesus turned and said to him, 'Get behind me Satan! You do not have in mind the concerns of God, but merely human concerns' (8:33). Jesus was not suggesting that Peter was demon-possessed, but rather that he was acting as a vehicle for temptation, as his mind was not focused on the need to rely on God for the truth about such matters. He was still operating within his own limited understanding and expectations, as seen again shortly afterwards, on the mountain of transfiguration, when he offers to build shelters for Jesus, Moses and Elijah, when they appear together (Mk. 9:2–13). Mark comments in 9:6, 'He did not know what to say, they were so frightened.' So Peter had reflected on the cause of his verbal gaffs, and wanted Mark to include them in his story of Christian origins, despite the fact that they portray Peter as, at one time, acting as an obstacle to the progress of the gospel. Surely that was because he had, with hindsight, come to understand the nature of the spiritual opposition with which he had engaged in combat. The devil and his forces of evil are able to put thoughts in a person's mind, and words in his mouth, and if they can do that with individuals, they can certainly infiltrate human groups and organizational structures. They can, in other words, influence the direction which people together take – in civil society, politics, and community groups, as well as in the church.

From this we can see that Peter's allusion to 'authorities and powers' is by no means a digression from his main theme, and that, therefore, we have to understand that his treatment of authoritarianism in 5:1–5 is part of his strategy of exposing evil in individual Christians, in the community of faith, and in the pagan world around. 'Lording it' is a pattern of behaviour, therefore, which Peter understands to be rooted in the machinations of the devil. It is no surprise to Peter that high-handed authoritarianism can become entrenched in church structures, as it can in the fabric of civil society, and in the corridors of stately power. Because of that, Christians are warned to be on the lookout for that kind of behaviour in the church, and to stamp it out.

In the same way, Peter's fellow apostle, James, had urged his people to 'Submit yourselves to God. Resist the devil and he will flee from you' (Jas. 4:7). But this follows an extensive discussion about the abuse of the tongue by church elders, in chapter 3, which begins with the advice, 'Not many of you should presume to be teachers, my brothers and sisters, because you know that we who teach will be judged more strictly' (Jas. 3:1). James explains what he means in some detail. The tongue may be small, but it can make great boasts, and, like the rudder of a ship, can change the course we take in life, as individuals and in fellowship with others. In the same way as a spark causes a forest fire, abuse of the tongue can destroy one's sense of direction in life. The tongue is potentially poisonous and evidently evil. With the tongue we can praise God and curse fellow human beings (3:3–12). The tongue can be a vehicle for bitter envy and selfish ambition, warns James (3:14), but where does all this evil ultimately originate? In his first chapter, James has faced up to the weakness of people under temptation, and tells them not to blame God for their own evil desires (1:13–15). But now he decides to name the powers which are behind such negative attitudes and actions. Christian leaders should demonstrate their wisdom and understanding, by living good lives in all humility, rather than by worldly wisdom, which 'does not come down from heaven, but is earthly, unspiritual, demonic. For where you have envy and selfish ambition, there you find disorder and every evil practice' (3:15–16).

We can now see the similarities between Peter and James in their treatment of this crucial issue. When we look holistically at their letters, we see how the problem of domineering behaviour by church leaders is of massive concern to the apostolic teams. The situation in the early churches is volatile, and human pride can lead to quarrels and fights, and push out humble prayer, so that intercessions and petitions remain unanswered by God. Why? 'You ask with wrong motives,' accuses James (Jas. 4:3; cf. 1 Pet. 3:6). Like Peter, he is chiefly concerned to persuade and motivate his hearers, and to shock them into facing up to the dreadful situations of which he has come to know, where professing believers are slandering one another (4:11) and perhaps even taking one another to court (4:12), while wealthier Christians are exploiting those who are poorer (5:1–6) and living lives of comparative luxury and self-indulgence.

For an appreciation of the apostolic use of the term authorities (*exousiai*) with regard to evil spiritual powers, we need to examine, first of all, the teaching of Paul in Ephesians, which was written to one of the key house church groupings in the province of Asia, to which Peter's circle later sent 1 Peter. We immediately see the common ground between Peter and Paul when we compare 1 Peter 3:22, 'Jesus Christ, who has gone into heaven and is at God's right hand – with angels, authorities and powers in submission to him' with Ephesians 1:20–21, '. . . the mighty strength he exerted when he raised Christ from the dead and seated him at his right hand in the heavenly realms, far above all rule and authority, power and dominion, and every name that can be invoked, not only in the present age but also in the one to come.' Here, scholars generally agree that Paul is referring not to human rulers and political structures, but to personal, supernatural powers.[8] Probably, both good and evil powers are connoted here, but the emphasis is clearly on the latter, as Paul later refers to the devil as 'the ruler of the kingdom (*exousias*) of the air' (Eph. 2:2), and *exousia* is used unequivocally of evil spirits in the famous spiritual warfare passage in Ephesians 6:12. From Paul's perspective, these 'authorities' are evil powers, which are enemies of Christ, yet are already, in some significant way, under the rule of Christ, so that believers need not be terrorized by their tyranny. Again, in Ephesians 3:10, after speaking about his vocation to preach the gospel to the non-Jewish world, Paul says, 'His intent was that now, through the church, the manifold wisdom of God should be made known to the rulers and authorities (*exousiais*) in the heavenly realms.' Paul means that 'the church by its very existence as a community consisting of both Jews and Gentiles is a testimony to God's salvific purposes'.[9] Paul views these authorities as intelligent beings which have limited knowledge, in that they were made aware of God's purposes only by the work of the apostles to bring together Jew and non-Jew, which is a foretaste of God's grand plan of cosmic reconciliation. So, at the climax of his great Ephesian epistle, Paul writes, 'For our struggle is not against flesh and blood, but against the rulers, against the authorities (*exousias*), against the powers of this dark world (*tous kosmokratōras tou skotous toutou*) and against the spiritual forces of evil in the heavenly realms' (Eph. 6:12).

This echoes the teaching of the apostle John about 'the darkness' in his prologue to the gospel: 'The light shines in the darkness, but the darkness has not overcome it' (Jn. 1:5). John illustrates Jesus' struggles with evil by using the antithesis of light and dark: 'You are going to have the light just a little while longer. Walk while you have the light, before darkness overtakes you. Those who walk in the dark do not know where they are going. Put your trust in the light while you have the light, so that you may become children of light' (Jn. 12:35–6). Paul expounded this theme in Ephesians 5:8–21:

> For you were once darkness, but now you are light in the Lord. Live as children of light (for the fruit of the light consists in all goodness, righteousness and truth) and find out what pleases the Lord. Have nothing to do with the fruitless deeds of darkness, but rather expose them. It is shameful even to mention what the disobedient do in secret. But everything exposed by the light becomes visible – and everything that is illuminated becomes a light . . . Be very careful, then, how you live – not as unwise but as wise, making the most of every opportunity, because the days are evil. Therefore do not be foolish, but understand what the Lord's will is . . . Submit to one another out of reverence for Christ.

Christian living – struggle is standard

Evil days, characterized by moral and spiritual 'darkness', demand very careful attention by Christians, both to opportune timing and to obedient trust, in other words. This will involve respecting proper authority in the church and approaching one another with the characteristic Christian attitude of mutual submission, out of reverence for Christ, who did not insist on his own way, but gave up his position of equality with God in order to serve his people and to save others from sin, yet was exalted to the highest place in the cosmos (see Phil. 2:1–11). In this way, despite what Paul says in Ephesians 1:20–21 about Christ's exaltation over all spiritual authorities, Ephesians 6:12 demonstrates that believers are still at war with evil powers. Although they are ultimately in subjection to Christ, these powers continue to oppose God's purposes, and try to overpower and disable God's people. There is no hint of triumphalism in Paul's teaching here, but rather a recognition of the reality faced every day by the churches as they struggle with unseen forces which are arrayed against them and remain a serious threat to their corporate health and safety.

Yet this struggle is not to be understood in a dualistic way. It is not a matter of good versus evil, as equals and opposites, where the outcome is uncertain. On the contrary, as we have noted, the sides are by no means equal in power or authority. The novels of Frank Peretti have done a disservice to the gospel when they have given the impression that believers should be obsessed by the activities of demonic powers behind the scenes of life, and so live in fear of evil.[10] It is true that evil forces, by their very nature and raison d'être, manage to deceive people and to conceal their real identity, because, as Paul says elsewhere, the devil poses as an angel of light[11] and uses impostor 'apostles' to infiltrate the church, distract believers, and distort the message. Paul certainly does not specify how evil powers may attack believers, individually and corporately, and does not use protognostic methods to equip his hearers for battle.[12] But Sydney Page suggests far too narrow a conception of temptation when he says there is good reason to believe that such opposition is primarily within the religio-ethical sphere. We must not limit spiritual warfare to the individualistic avoidance of sexual immorality, impurity and greed, despite Paul's focus on these evils in Ephesians 5:3. After all, as Walter Wink has argued, the powers of evil inhabit authorities in the real world, as well as infiltrating the church:

> I developed the thesis that undergirds all three volumes of the work: that the NT's 'principalities and powers' is a generic category referring to the determining forces of physical, psychic, and social existence. These powers usually consist of an outer manifestation, and an inner spirituality or interiority. Power must become incarnate, institutionalised, or systemic, in order to be effective. It has a dual aspect, possessing both an outer, visible form (constitutions, judges, police, leaders, office complexes) and an inner, invisible spirit that provides it legitimacy, compliance, credibility, and clout.[13]

Peter and James exhort all believers, and particularly Christian leaders, to resist the devil (1 Pet. 5:9; Jas. 4:7). This connects with Paul's call to expose the works of darkness and take a stand against evil powers (Eph. 5:11; 6:11). But how is this resistance to be effected? Peter says, 'You [plural] resist him by being firm in faith.'[14] The sense of 'faith' is not, here, about assent to doctrine, but expresses the idea of personal or communal commitment of trust, as God is trustworthy (cf. 1 Pet. 1:5, 7, 9, 21; 4:21). While non-resistance, rather than tit for tat retaliation, is advocated by Jesus in relation to a disciplined Christian response to personal abuse by an evil person (Mt. 5:39), such passivity is not to be the approach vis-à-vis spiritual evil, which is the ultimate source of such opposition. Peter says that 'disobedient spirits' (1 Pet. 3:19) are behind those who reject and denounce Christ, who, as Paul says, may well be unaware that they are the hapless tools of Satan.[15] While Peter commands his flock to be respectful of and submissive to all legitimate human authorities (1 Pet. 2:13–17), there is to be no deference to the devil! As Michaels notes, 'To resist the devil is not to engage in hostile actions against anyone, but to trust God.'[16]

Yet this does not mean being devoid of guile and strategy in handling the devil's human agents, whose destructive influence must be neutralized if the gospel is to penetrate human minds and cultures. A key to this struggle, according to Peter, is recognizing that all Christians are universally subject to the sufferings caused by the evil machinations of the devil and his heavenly and earthly messengers. In fact, their struggles are a necessary part of God's purposes for the cosmos (5:9)[17] and occur wherever and whenever Christian communities take seriously their commitment to Christ.[18]

That's why, thirty years later, the apostle John warned Christians in the Asian cities of Smyrna and Philadelphia about the 'Synagogue of Satan' (Rev. 2:9; 3:9), which seems to refer to the continuing organized Jewish communities in those places, which were apparently opposing the Messianic claims of Christ and his church. The devil was testing believers through that negative influence (2:10), and also through the pagan idolaters in nearby Pergamum, 'where Satan has his throne . . . where Satan lives' (2:13). Again, believers in Asian Thyatira were warned about the Gnostic cults in which initiates were shown 'Satan's so-called deep secrets' (2:24). These evil authorities and powers had to be exposed and overcome – but how? The Exalted Lord says, through John, 'Repent, therefore! Otherwise, I will soon come to you and will fight against them with the sword of my mouth' (2:16). The first priority is to get rid of sin within the churches themselves, which means giving up rebellious beliefs and behaviour in order to avoid being on the wrong side in the spiritual struggle. Again, Paul had earlier equipped the Ephesian house churches with the full armour of God for their ongoing spiritual warfare, using the analogy of Roman infantry in battle readiness (Eph. 6:13–18), prepared to withstand the onslaught of rebellious or insurgent elements, rather than engaging in empire-building expansion.

This resonates with Peter's call to resistance (1 Pet. 5:9), which means withstanding rather than fighting against. It implies that the enemy employs surprise tactics, akin to modern guerrilla warfare and terrorism, which necessitate the appropriate defensive and counter-offensive measures, and that such outbreaks of hostility are seasonal rather than unremitting. Paul says, 'Therefore, put on the full armour of God, so that when the day of evil comes, you may be able to stand your ground, and after you have done everything, to stand' (Eph. 6:13). The body armour was attached to a leather belt and kilt, and strong sandals with studded soles were essential parts of the kit, as was the large shield, behind which the phalanxes of legionnaires progressed slowly against all that was being thrown at them by their enemies. Above all, they needed the protection of their helmets, and the weapon of the short sword, which was used for close-quarter engagement. In this way, Paul calls the Ephesians to 'Take the sword of the Spirit, which is the word of God, and pray in the Spirit on all occasions, with all kinds of prayers and requests. With this in mind, be alert and always keep on praying for all the Lord's people' (Eph. 6:17b–18). Jesus the Lord, as commander-in-chief, exercises his supreme authority through faithful witness to his message, in other words, through ministers of the word and gospel-gossips, who are empowered by the prayers of God's people. Paul concludes, 'Pray also for me, that whenever I speak, words may be given me so that I will fearlessly make known the mystery of the gospel' (6:19). This is the way Christians are to resist the devil with all his usurped authority and power.

A closer look at *exousia* – and demonic domineering

Before we draw this chapter to a close, we must look more closely at the Greek noun *exousia* ('authority', 'ruling power, 'bearer of authority'). The misuse of authority is also defined by the use of the verb *katexousiazein* ('to exercise authority over', 'to misuse official authority', 'to tyrannize'). In classical thought, the noun implied the unrestricted possibility or freedom of action, from which follows the idea of right of action, or authority. *Exousia* denotes the power which may be demonstrated in legal, political, social, or moral affairs, and it is always linked with a particular position or mandate. Such authority can be delegated, and may also be illegally usurped by despots. The phrase 'the authorities' therefore reflects this usage, and means those who are, legally or by usurpation, exercising official power.[19]

In the Septuagint, *exousia* occurs only fifty times, and one of the most significant usages, which helps us to understand the New Testament meaning of the word, is found in the book of Daniel, where the authority of human world rulers is thought to originate from the supernatural realm. It is delegated by God, who is the Lord of history, and whose rule is eternal (Dan. 4:31). He installs and removes kings (2:21), and can take away their dominion from them (7:12). Daniel 7 grounds the unsatisfactory and provisional nature of all human government in the dominion of chaotic powers, which are opposed to God, and in their denial of God's delegation of responsibility to them. Because of this, at the end of the times, and at the lowest point in the history of human rule, the 'Son of Man' will be enthroned and invested with might, glory, and sovereign authority to rule all nations. His dominion will be an everlasting dominion, which will never pass away (7:14). This corporate personality figure, according to 7:27, represents 'the people of the saints of the Most High', the true Israel of the last days. They shall receive kingly power, and all rulers will obey them. Later Jewish interpreters developed this and equated the 'Son of Man' concept with the final judge of the world or with the Messiah himself.

In the New Testament, *exousia* is found 108 times. Otto Betz explains: '*Exousia* is that power, authority, and freedom of action which belongs (1) to God himself; (2) to a commission in the last days; and (3) to a Christian in his eschatological existence.'[20] We look at each of these points in turn.

The first area links God's ultimate authority with his role as the Lord of history, through which he has fixed the dates and times and has the ultimate end of history in his control (Acts 1:7). He has the power to send people to eternal perdition (Lk. 12:5). Paul compares God to a potter, who can do what he wishes with his lump of clay (Rom. 9:21; cf. Isa. 29:16). God is well able to delegate his authority, yet the heavenly authorities are under the subjection of the exalted Christ (Eph. 1:21; 1 Pet. 3:22). Those which continue to oppose God's purposes are nevertheless still under the overall authority of the Messiah (1 Cor. 15:24). All human beings are born into a world which suffers, to a large extent, from mismanagement and misrule, at the earthly and heavenly levels, so that there is a dominion of darkness and the devil (Col. 1:13; Acts 16:18), which stands against the kingdom of light, the reign of God. However, the devil seems to have much more power, in some New Testament sources, than this theology would allow. For example, in the Gospel of John he is called 'the ruler of this world' (Jn. 12:31; 14:30; 16:11), and in 2 Corinthians 'the god of this world' (2 Cor. 4:4), and is said to have powers of delegation to his minions, such as the Antichrist (Rev. 13:2, etc.). And the devil tempted Jesus with a delusional offer of sovereignty over nations on his behalf (Lk. 4:6). Yet the devil's activity always fits in with God's ultimate purposes, and his evil schemes are therefore limited in power and duration (Lk. 22:53). As Betz notes, 'Statements about the power of the devil are not to be assigned a place in the pessimistic view of the world, but in the Good News of the redemptive work of Christ. It is precisely where Jesus speaks of the devil as the "prince of this world" that he announces his downfall.'[21]

The second area Betz mentions has to do with the fact that Jesus has been given *exousia*, in a special way. His earthly ministry uniquely heralds the coming of God's reign, and announces that evil powers have been dealt with definitively in his life, death and resurrection. The Son of God has been sent into the world by the Father, with authority to destroy the works of the devil, and to deliver people from his dominion. Exorcism is therefore attributed to the authority of Jesus (Lk. 4:36), which he can delegate to his disciples (Mt. 10:1ff). Jesus acted with God's authority when he forgave sins and confirmed the promise with miraculous healings (Mk. 2:3–12; 5:1–43; 7:24–37; 8:22–30). Above all, this authority was seen in Jesus' teaching, which often provoked amazement from his hearers (Mk. 1:22, 27), because he did not teach like the scribes of his day, who were guided by their rabbinic traditions (Mt. 7:29); he not only spoke the very words of God, like Moses and the prophets, but taught with the unique authority of God's Son, who alone knows the Father and can reveal his inmost thoughts. However, it is the resurrection which establishes forever Jesus' authority, as Mt. 28:18 reminds us, where Christ claims to have been given all power in heaven and on earth, so that he can commission his followers to take his message to the ends of the earth. This vision fulfilled Daniel's apocalyptic insights into the enthronement and granting of sovereignty to the Son of Man, but the collective 'saints of the Most High' is now fulfilled in the exalted Christ. Furthermore, God's authority is not realized by the violent subjugation of the nations, but by the permeation of the gospel of the Kingdom,[22] through which the world will be won to faith in Christ. In this way, the church is the principal outward expression of the rule of the Messiah on earth (Acts 1:6–8); yet the church is not to be equated with God's Kingdom, which is a much wider dynamic concept covering God's reign in relation to every aspect of human endeavour and network. The cross and the exaltation of Jesus Christ demonstrate that the evil spiritual authorities have been definitively disarmed in a mighty act of judgment, at the turning point of history. This good news must be preached to all the world, and the exalted Lord empowers his ambassadors to proclaim the gospel.

Thirdly, in terms of Betz's explanation, this implies that all Christian believers, and not just leaders, have a delegated authority, founded on the reign of Christ as Lord and his disarming of the powers of evil, which entails a vocation of both freedom and service. As Martin Luther famously said, 'A Christian is a perfectly free lord of all, subject to none. A Christian is a perfectly dutiful servant to all, subject to all.'[23] The believer is free to do anything (1 Cor. 6:12; 10:23), because, now that Christ has been exalted, nothing is under the rule of the powers. Yet this theoretically limitless freedom is qualified by compassionate Christian consideration of what may be helpful to others, in view of the fact that the full redemption is still to come (1 Cor. 6:12; 10:13). People should therefore be sensible, and take into account both their own Christian lives and the experience of those who may, as yet, be weaker in faith (1 Cor. 10:28), rather than exercise the unbridled liberty of the children of God, which can be enjoyed only beyond the end of time, in the resurrection life of the new heavens and earth (cf. Rom. 8:18–25). In fact, such an unrestrained use of one's liberty could lead a believer into a new form of slavery. Paul says, 'I have the right to do anything, but I will not be mastered (*exousiasthēsomai*) by anything' (1 Cor. 6:12). We can see from this that it is possible for professing Christians to become habitual control freaks who seek to dominate others in their exercise of proper authority in the church. They imagine that they are doing so according to the leadership powers which have been delegated to them, but they are, in reality, authority addicts.

Finally, to return to 1 Peter, we can now appreciate more fully the concern of Peter and his associates to deal with the problem of authoritarianism in the churches of Asia Minor, and how that concern can be expressed, for the contemporary and future health of the churches worldwide. Good Christian leadership is the key to balanced growth of faithful lifestyles and effective communication of the gospel. There is only one Lord, Jesus Christ, and those who 'lord it' over Christian congregations or agencies are usurping his authority, just as the heavenly and earthly powers of evil have done throughout history. All authorities, both spiritual and political, are ultimately in submission to the risen Lord (1 Pet. 3:22), who delegates his authority to them for their growth as human beings as well as for the wider commonwealth. Yet, as Lord Acton famously lamented, 'Power tends to corrupt, and absolute power corrupts absolutely.'[24] There are great temptations awaiting all who seek to become teachers and leaders within the churches, and they are held especially accountable to God for the proper exercise of their powers. They dare not mimic the work of the devil and dominate God's dear ones, but rather must follow Christ's example of servant-leadership and face up to the reality that 'Power must become incarnate, institutionalised, or systemic', as Walter Wink says.[25] Or as M. Scott Peck suggests, 'Satan has no power except in a human body . . . In fact, the only power that Satan has is through human belief in its lies.'[26] Because of that we must be very vigilant to ensure that ultimately our only model for leadership and management is the incarnate Lord, and we will be exploring how that can be possible in the twenty-first century in the remainder of this book. In so doing we will seek to discover the true source of the 'legitimacy, compliance, credibility, and clout'[27] which will surely be the outcomes of a renewal of real Christian leading and leadership styles in today's churches. But before we complete our dialogue with Peter and his associates, we must focus finally on their call to true Christian humility in 1 Peter 5:6–7.

Summary

Let's summarize where this important chapter has taken our discussion:

- Walter Wink and Scott Peck have enabled a renewed contemporary awareness of the reality of evil powers and their influence in individual lives and in ecclesiastical and societal structures.
- Peter offers a parallel treatment of spiritual warfare which enhances the Pauline strand of teaching.
- Evil is to be overcome through prayer and Christ-like attitudes and actions, but believers should expect ongoing spiritual struggles as part and parcel of their Christian life and witness.
- Peter's focus on the misuse of authority in the world and in the church is related to his understanding of the work of demonic powers.

7

Under God's Hand

We have seen that authoritarian leadership styles are not an option for elders/overseers (today's pastors, priests, ministers, bishops and senior executives of Christian agencies), according to the apostolic appeal in 1 Peter, because Christian leaders who lord it over God's people are succumbing to the schemes of Satan, as well as failing to model their ministry on the servant-leadership style of Christ, the Chief Shepherd. In contrast to authoritarian approaches, good leaders are also followers, who willingly submit to their fellow-believers out of reverence for Christ (Eph. 5:21), and faithfully respond to Peter's paraenesis: 'All of you, clothe yourselves with humility toward one another, because "God opposes the proud but shows favour to the humble and oppressed." Humble yourselves, therefore, under God's mighty hand, that he may lift you up in due time' (1 Pet. 5:5b–6).

Not only had humility been fleshed out before Peter's eyes in the person and work of Christ, it was also a virtue which was highly valued in the Jewish community out of which Peter came. He quotes here from Proverbs 3:34, rather than from any of the sayings of Jesus (which he was probably compiling at that time with Mark for his gospel), but the imagery of clothing oneself with humility is clearly drawn from Peter's experience as a participant at the Last Supper, when Jesus literally took the role of a servant and washed his disciples' feet, much to Peter's chagrin (Jn. 13:4). Norman Hillyer comments on the vividness of the metaphorical language here in 1 Peter:

> The picture is of donning a slave's apron, tied on tightly so as to leave the body free for action. 'Do not use humility as the usual

loose-fitting garment, so readily put on or taken off according to
whim, but as a close-fitting overall intended for work and wear.'
Humility is a matter not of downcast eyes, or of the mentality of a
Uriah Heep ('I'm only an 'umble clerk, Mr Copperfield'), but of
active selfless service toward one another.[1]

Humility and selfism

However, we who are reading the New Testament in today's
Westernized societies may feel alienated by the hyperbolic language that Peter uses here. After all, we live in a culture which
values self-assertion and self-realization, rather than humility,
and where we may even find ourselves subject to attempted
domination by certain leaders to whom the psychiatrist Paul Vitz
refers as 'fascist-authoritarian' types.[2] Vitz contrasts selfism (as
exemplified in the *Sesame Street* saying from children's television:
'The most important person in the whole wide world is you, and
you hardly even know you!'[3]) with the basic teaching of Jesus on
self-worth: 'Blessed are the meek, for they will inherit the earth'
(Mt. 5:5).[4] Selfism is ultimately about 'winning through intimidation'[5] and, sadly, it can readily be found in Christian circles today,
as well as in the secular context. Vitz believes that we have all
been influenced by modern humanistic self-psychology, which
he calls 'the cult of self-worship' and which, he asserts, is at odds
with historic Christian faith and lifestyle. 'The idea of love as
involving self-sacrifice and submission to a higher loyalty will
strike the therapeutic sensibility as intolerably oppressive.'[6]

Why should this be, if we agree with Vitz? A belief currently
prevails that every impulse should be gratified, and that we can
find satisfaction and happiness as humans only if our needs for
self-realization are met. In fact, Michael Moynagh, a recent British
proponent of the so-called Emerging Church movement, argues
that churches in the Western world need to take cognizance of
what he calls the 'new consumerism', or 'It-must-fit-me-world'.
Driven by globalization, postmodern values, demographics and
technology, this new mindset is allegedly making headway in
society and church. We wealthy Westerners can purchase new
cars with all the specifications that we as individuals require,

including a personalized number plate. We can hope for a church which will suit our temperament and needs, and that of our families, and move when we don't fit in or feel frustrated. How will that attitude affect Christian thinking and practice which has traditionally focused on believers' willingness to fit in with the needs of others? Moynagh argues that we need a fresh approach:

> By and large, the church is still stuck in the standardized world. It approaches evangelism with a mass mindset. 'Come and join our church' is the invitation, which assumes that 'our church' is suitable for the people we invite. 'We like it so other people will.' That is typical one-size-fits-all thinking. The church could get away with it in mass society, but in a must-fit-me world it won't wash any more. A different approach is needed – one that is more sensitive to the differences between people, to their suspicion of organizations and to their expectation of choice. The reaction of other organizations is to draw closer to people, to listen to them and to respond to their individual preferences. Can the church afford to stand aloof?[7]

Yet destructive aggression is a natural propensity in people, from birth, and cannot be filtered out of the cries for the satisfaction of personal aspirations and desires.[8] Psychiatrist and author M. Scott Peck therefore exposes this double-think and describes its proponents as 'the people of the lie'.[9] It is simply nonsense to imagine that we can have all our felt needs met in this way, as in the craving of the Queen hit song 'I want it all, and I want it now!' The truth lies in the very opposite direction, according to the teaching of Jesus, who turns upside down contemporary popular lifestyle philosophies and psychologies of self-worth.

Peter lived in an age of self-aggrandizement and empire-building, and wrote his first circular letter from Rome to the churches in the provinces of Asia Minor, which were gatherings of people who lived in territories occupied by the armed forces of their imperial overlords. He could have used current secular and religious models as examples of good leadership, but had only one example for his people to follow: Jesus Christ, the unique Son of God, who had humbled himself for a time, and had been exalted to his Father's right hand. Mark's Gospel clearly contains many of Peter's reminiscences of Jesus' life and teaching, which illustrate the theme of leadership through radical humility. Let's look at some key passages.

Lose-Win

Mark 1:7 refers to John the Baptist's humble message about the Messiah, who was about to be manifested to God's people: 'After me comes the one more powerful than I, the thongs of whose sandals I am not worthy to stoop down and untie.' Yet Jesus would never treat others as a master treated slaves in those days, despite his claims to ultimate authority over all human life, proclaiming that 'The Kingdom of God has come near' (1:15). Filled with compassion, Jesus reached out and touched a despised leper so that he might be healed (1:41), and he openly claimed to have authority on earth to forgive sins (2:10). Those who came to him for healing and forgiveness were happy to confess that they were sinners who were morally and spiritually sick, and in need of a pastoral doctor (2:17). That required a good deal of humility. Eventually, Jesus began to teach his disciples that he would suffer many things, and be rejected by the religious leaders before being killed and rising to new life. He would suffer humiliation, predicted Jesus, but Peter would have none of it (8:31–32). In response, Jesus took the opportunity to address the crowd as well as his disciples:

> Whoever wants to be my disciple must deny themselves and take up their cross and follow me. For whoever wants to save their life will lose it, but whoever loses their life for me and for the gospel will save it. What good is it for you to gain the whole world, yet forfeit your soul? (8:34–36)

Despite this affirmation, Jesus' disciples still argued openly about who among them was the greatest when they were en route to Peter's home in Capernaum, and the Lord had to deal with their lack of humility in the manner of a Jewish rabbi of the time, sitting down as a teacher with his class, and saying, 'Anyone who

wants to be first, must be the very last, and the servant of all'
(9:35). Yet, not long afterwards, the brothers James and John
approached Jesus and asked him to let them be in the top positions of prestige and power when his kingdom was established.
'You don't know what you're asking,' Jesus retorted, implying
that to be so close to him would mean enduring the kind of suffering he was about to experience, but the other disciples, including Peter, were very annoyed with the two 'Sons of Thunder' for
their arrogance. Again, 'rabbi' Jesus called them together and
rammed home his point:

> You know that those who are regarded as rulers of the Gentiles
> lord it over them, and their high officials exercise authority over
> them. Not so with you. Instead, whoever wants to become great
> among you must be your servant, and whoever wants to be first
> must be slave of all. For even the Son of man did not come to be
> served but to serve, and to give his life as a ransom for many
> (10:35–45).

Here is what Tom Wright, Bishop of Durham, has to say about
this crucial text:

> The cross is not, for Jesus or for Mark, a difficult episode to be got
> through on the way to a happy ending. It is precisely God's way
> of standing worldly power and authority on its head. When, at the
> end of this passage, Jesus quotes the servant song ('. . . to give his
> life a ransom for many'), he is making the point, with which Isaiah
> would have emphatically agreed, that the kingdom of God turns
> the world's ideas of power and glory upside down and inside
> out.[10] . . . The cross calls into question all human pride and glory.[11]
> . . . Jesus is going up to Jerusalem, turning the world's values on
> their heads, setting off to give his life as a ransom for many. If we
> want to receive what he has to offer, we have no choice but to fol-
> low.[12]

Such language sounds very strange to modern ears, yet this is
what makes the gospel good news. It was as fresh and challenging
to aspiring leaders in Peter's day, thirty years after the crucifixion
of Christ, as it is to us today – because it seems to be advocating

leadership styles which cannot possibly work in the real world, so critics maintain. The thought that Christian leaders might have to retrain their whole way of thinking about appropriate management methods has always been too radical for most even to begin to attempt.[13] It's far easier to go with the flow, and conform to the worldly wisdom of the latest popular theorist, in order to give the impression that the church is keeping up with the times. The problem is that much of contemporary management theory is, as I shall demonstrate, fatally flawed and potentially destructive of healthy organizational cultures.

But all is not lost, as Paul Vitz reminds us, and God has not been left without his witnesses in the psychological and business worlds, which so influence current Christian leadership praxis. There are avenues of hope which can encourage concerned believers to find recovery from domineering leadership, and hope even for those who have fallen into negative patterns of organizational behaviour to find release. Strangely enough, there are some psychological theories and practices which have not bowed the knee to 'Ba'alism'.[14] One such is CBT, Cognitive Behavioural Therapy. Paul Vitz concludes, in his critique of self-ism as the underpinning philosophy, which informs much of modern psychology, that there is another way to deal with many of the emotional and behavioural phenomena which typify current crises in human organizational relationships, interpersonal dilemmas, and individual mental suffering. He says this: 'There is some evidence that cognitive-behavioural methods, when applied to very specific psychological problems – for example, phobias, panic attacks, etc. – can be superior to the various forms of "talk" therapy. (But these approaches are not part of humanistic self-psychology).'[15]

We will take time to explore the implications of this exciting prospect in the next chapter. But we must understand that the influence of selfist philosophy is all-pervasive in our Westernized cultures. It informs educational theory, for example, in the project of Values Clarification in Education: 'The proponents want students to overcome apathy, over conformity, flightiness, etc., and to acquire purposeful, proud, positive and enthusiastic behaviour patterns.'[16] But that makes the assumption that such behaviour is to be valued as good in itself. Yet, as Vitz wryly comments, 'Hitler and Stalin were certainly purposeful, proud, and enthusiastic.'[17]

Selfism is such a problem in organizations because it never comes to grips with the question of who or what is ultimately responsible for society, and promotes 'a chamber of commerce economic growth philosophy of mental life'.[18] The sad thing is that within the Reformed and evangelical churches, humanistic philosophy and psychology became entrenched in the twentieth century. Paul Vitz was brought up in Protestant circles, but later converted to Roman Catholicism, and he gives among his reasons the following:

> Such traditional spiritual concepts as . . . prayer, contemplation, obedience, repentance and mysticism . . . became so weak in mainline twentieth-century Protestantism as to be of little significance. The notion of pride as the fundamental sin, along with greed, envy, etc., yielded to the belief that the fundamental sin is to be chaotic and unfocused.[19]

You may recall that in one of our six stories (case studies) in chapter 2, despite the fact that George was very organized and extremely focused, he developed a domineering style of leadership which was not characterized by Christian humility. Yet he was quite pious and theologically conservative, and increasingly wished to be associated with those who sought to defend and promote the historic Reformed Christian faith and saw themselves as the faithful followers of the evangelical revivals of the eighteenth and nineteenth centuries. Should that be a surprise to us? Pietism, after all, includes an 'emphasis on intense emotional response, usually occurring in small groups, but sometimes involving larger revival meetings',[20] and historically was a reaction to rigid, intellectualistic and authoritarian forms of religion. The Methodist class system and circuit ministry models were the result of the Wesleys' concern to encourage heart-warming fellowship and worship in the congregations they planted and supported. John Wesley had become all too aware of the dangers of authoritarian Christian leadership when he was forbidden by some Anglican bishops to engage in field preaching during his many evangelistic tours.

Authoritarianism was not novel in the eighteenth century, nor was it in New Testament times. Vitz notes: 'Christians from the beginning have been aware of the problems of excessive institutionalized authority and the dangers of bad faith that it can create.'[21] That is why Peter exhorts all believers to 'Humble yourselves under God's mighty hand' (1 Pet. 5:6), where humility means submission to God's care and protection, following Proverbs 3:34: 'God shows favour to the humble and oppressed.' Luke relates Jesus' parable of the wedding guests, in Luke 14:11, which illustrates Jesus' teaching on true humility. He had noticed how the guests picked places of honour at the reception, but that it was best to wait until the host invited them to take an appropriate place, rather than be humiliated in being asked to step down. The punchline of the parable is, 'For all those who exalt themselves will be humbled, and those who humble themselves will be   exalted' (14:11). The same conclusion is affirmed in Luke 18:14, at the end of the parable of the Pharisee and the tax collector, in a specifically religious context. Matthew 23:12 contains the same warning, in the middle of Jesus' attack on the false piety of the Jewish religious leaders, so it was clearly an important part of his preaching, and tackled a very real danger faced by his own followers. In effect, he is warning us not to follow the leadership styles which are prevalent in contemporary culture, but only to follow his way. That is why, in Matthew 18:4, Jesus says to his disciples, 'Therefore, whoever takes a humble place – becoming like this child – is the greatest in the kingdom of heaven' in answer to their question about where true greatness lies. Paul's hymn to Christ as Lord in Philippians 2:8 shows how humility became an important theme in early Christian worship and theology– 'And being found in appearance as a human being, he humbled himself by becoming obedient to death – even death on a cross!' Why, then, is humility such a strange concept for many Christians today?

There is no doubt that, in reaction to the widespread confusion about Christian belief which resulted from the movement of theological liberalism in the late nineteenth and early twentieth centuries, some orthodox Christian leaders adopted authoritarian approaches to ministry and leadership in the churches. Some even came to believe that if they were faithful to the apostolic doctrines they should exercise a similar authority over the congregations which they served, and should be respected and obeyed as the apostles were in New Testament times. This bred a sycophancy which is characterized by the phenomenon of the 'human doormat', for, as Vitz tellingly comments, 'No Christian can adore or blindly submit to any other human being.'[22]

Every believer a priest

Rather than developing high-handed and underhand ways of freakishly controlling congregations and organizations, Christian leaders are called, especially, to live under God's mighty hand, with the humility of Christ, as the apostle Peter enjoins. The metaphor of God's 'mighty hand' used here is rooted in the theme of deliverance in the Hebrew scriptures. Moses, in the fifteenth century BCE, was assured by the LORD that the elders of Israel would listen to him and that together they would confront Pharaoh, and ask him to let the Israelites return to Canaan. Yet God said, 'But I know that the king of Egypt will not let you go unless a mighty hand compels him' (Ex. 3:19; cf. 6:1; Deut. 7:8; 9:26). The psalmist also rejoiced in the goodness of God the deliverer, whose love endures forever, when he recalled that 'He brought Israel out from among the Egyptians, with a mighty hand and outstretched arm' (Ps. 136:11–12). Again, Nehemiah, exiled in Persia (modern Iran) in the fifth century BCE, prayed to the LORD to repeat his feats of deliverance in his own day: 'Remember the instruction you gave your servant Moses . . . if your exiled people are at the farthest horizon, I will gather them from there . . . They are your servants and your people, whom you redeemed by your great strength and your mighty hand' (Neh. 1:8–10).

Christopher Wright shows that Peter's understanding of the ethos of both ecclesiastical leadership and political kingship is rooted in the teaching of Deuteronomy, and connects that with the theme of this book:

> In his submission to the law, the king must not consider himself better than his brothers, even though he has been set over them in

political terms. Functional authority must be exercised in a context of covenant equality . . . the model of leadership before us here is a challenge to those in Christian leadership in churches or parachurch organizations. Christians are as vulnerable to the temptations of power, prestige, and wealth as Israelite kings, and the warning of Jesus (Luke 22:24–27)[23] never loses its relevance[24] . . . The early church modeled itself on the Deuteronomic pattern of devolved leadership portrayed here[25] . . . The NT never calls those who serve the church in its leadership 'priests'. Priesthood is applied only to either Christ (Hebrews 7, etc.) or the whole community of believers (1 Peter 2:9, echoing the same collective use in Exodus 19:4–6).[26]

Tackling self-centredness

The rest of this book is devoted to a search for God's hand of deliverance for the Western churches in the twenty-first century, CE, through a recovery of catholic and apostolic leading paradigms. Paul Vitz encouragingly assures us that there is a way forward out of the mess in which many Christian leaders, and their congregations, currently find themselves: 'The only way out is to love the self, to let it go, and once more willingly to become an object again . . . not an object to be controlled by other selves acting as subjects, but an object in the love and service of God.'[27] And the key is found, once more, in the teaching of Jesus Christ: 'Whoever takes a humble place – becoming like this child – is the greatest in the Kingdom' (Mt. 18:3–4). The New Testament is against 'the psychology of the independent, rebellious, autonomous, self-centred self.'[28] So Vitz concludes, as a converted Roman Catholic: 'We need sermons on radical obedience, on the mysticism of submissive surrender of the will . . . on how to find humility.'[29]

And of course, all those themes are found in 1 Peter. Right from the beginning, Peter congratulates his target audience that God has chosen them to be set apart by the Holy Spirit for the purpose of obedience to Jesus Christ (1:2), and the noun *hypakoē* is also used in 1:14 and 1:22: 'As obedient children, do not conform to the evil desires you had when you lived in ignorance . . . Now that you have purified yourselves by obeying the truth . . . love one another deeply, from the heart.' The concept of obedience in Greek is rooted in the notion of attentiveness and listening. The obedience which Peter encourages is the proper receptive response to the hearing of the gospel message, in other words, but it is also connected with the cleansing work of Christ on the cross and the holiness which is the goal of the gospel (1:2, 15). Christian leaders are called to be good listeners to the Lord as well as good listeners for the members of their congregations. Again, this is an area where CBT can be used – to develop listening skills. As David Burns notes:

> The three listening skills – disarming, empathy, and inquiry – capture the essence of effective listening. These skills are frequently overlooked, even by professionals whose very work demands expert communication. In a recent study at Presbyterian Medical Center in Denver, more than 300 clinical interviews by physicians were observed and evaluated. The investigators commented . . . Physicians at all levels (of training) who had previously been thought quite competent appeared defective in their interaction with patients . . . One of the problems: Doctors did not listen carefully to patients.[30]

One wonders what the results of a similar survey might be if it was carried out with ministers or priests. But the clear teaching of the New Testament is that we cannot be listening to God if we are not listening to people. Christian obedience, especially for leaders, involves two-way traffic. We cannot say that we love God if we don't love our fellow believers, for a start. 'For if we do not love a fellow believer, whom we have seen, we cannot love God, whom we have not seen' (1 Jn. 4:20). And Peter shows that true obedience is contrasted with that of those who refuse to obey: 'For it is time for judgment to begin with God's household; and if it begins with us, what will the outcome be for those who do not obey the gospel of God?' (1 Pet. 4:17). Disobedience cannot produce the character and commitment which God desires; obedience has certain outcomes which are crucial to the experience of salvation and in order to prepare for judgment.

This, as we have seen above, is light years away from the humanistic self-psychology which is so popular today, and also

makes Michael Moynagh's claims that the church should mould
its message to suit the 'must-fit-me world' seem strangely at odds
with historic Christianity. Yet an undue emphasis on obedience is
also to be avoided, according to the balanced presentation of
Peter. Excessive institutional authority is clearly not what the
apostle is advocating; nor is he encouraging blind submission or
sycophancy. However, we must not forget that his use of paraenetic methods in seeking to motivate his hearers is, in and of
itself, looking for true Christian obedience as a response. That's
why there are so many ethical imperatives in the letter, as we
have noted. To live in Christian obedience is to live humbly,
'under God's mighty hand' (1 Pet. 5:6). 'Clothe yourselves with
humility toward one another, because "God opposes the proud
but shows favour to the humble and oppressed"' (5:5). 'Finally,
all of you, be like-minded, be sympathetic, love one another, be
compassionate and humble' (3:8).

That implies a surrender of our wills to the divine priorities
which obedience recognizes. Living in obedience is part of the
mystical experience of union with Christ, rather than merely following orders, just as Sarah's obedience to her husband Abraham
was clearly a dynamic response of love towards somebody she
respected and admired, rather than feared (1 Pet. 3:6). It is an
aspect of the transformed relationships which are the result of the
work of the gospel in the power of the Spirit. And central to that
is the appropriate attitude of Christian leaders: 'Be shepherds of
God's flock . . . not because you must, but because you are willing' (5:2). Leading by example is the expression of humble obedience and surrendered wills. In the next chapter, we will continue
to explore holistic biblical and psychological resources which can
help us to find help and healing as Christian leaders and followers in the contemporary cultural climate of postmodernity.

Summary

Let's summarize this chapter's main points:

- Christian humility is the opposite of selfism, which tries to win
  through intimidation.

- Peter's letters, following his collaboration with Mark in his Gospel, teach radical humility.
- Leadership and authority in 1 Peter are rooted in the theology of Deuteronomy, the origin of the idea of the 'priesthood of all believers'.
- In contrast to the self-centred self, Christians are called to grow in love and service towards God and others. This can be encouraged through understanding and applying non-selfist therapies such as Cognitive Behavioural Therapy (CBT).

8

Mending Networks

In chapter 1 we alluded to the fact that, as a fisherman who was involved in a business co-operative, Simon Peter must have known a good deal about what we now call management, and must have been aware of the problems which every human organization has to address on a daily basis. He originally came from the Galilean village of Bethsaida (Aramaic, 'house of fishing'), where he worked in partnership with his brother Andrew, along with James and John, the sons of Zebedee (Lk. 5:7,10). It is no surprise, therefore, to find metaphorical language which is rooted in the fishing industry, both in Peter's letters and in Mark's Gospel, for which Peter was probably the principal source. For example, Mark records the calling of Jesus' first disciples by the Sea of Galilee, when the brothers Simon and Andrew were casting their nets into the waters of the lake (Mk. 1:16), using a circular casting net, which could be cast from a boat or while standing in shallow water. At the same time, James and John were in their boat, preparing their nets for the next fishing trip (1:19). The care of nets included washing, drying and mending, and it is significant, therefore, that in 1 Peter 5:10, when the author promises his addressees that 'The God of all grace . . . will himself restore you',[1] where restoration has the sense of 'making whole',[2] he uses the same Greek verb, *katartizein*, which Mark uses of mending nets in Mark 1:19, in a metaphorical sense. Norman Hillyer comments, 'The situation, spiritually speaking, is similar for all believers. After the wear and tear of daily living for God in a hostile environment, they need to be renewed, restored, and fully re-equipped.'[3]

Repairing wear and tear

This must be connected with what Peter has already said, in 1 Peter 5:7, about casting all our anxiety on God because he cares for us, which itself flows out of Peter's exhortation to humble ourselves under God's hand (5:6). The 'casting' envisaged here is not rooted in the technicalities of fishing at that time, but signifies a 'definite act of handing over the burden of anxiety'[4] to God, in the same way that the disciples threw clothing on the backs of the colt for Jesus' triumphal entry into Jerusalem (Lk. 19:35). The Greek word for anxiety here implies being pulled in different directions at once.[5] While this language is not directly connected with fishing, the net is certainly a piece of equipment which is constantly being pulled in different directions at the same time. The same is true of human networks, of which Christian churches are notable examples. Hillyer's imagination is not going too far, therefore, when he suggests that Peter was probably extending the analogy of his experience as a fisherman to dealing with the kind of tensions and stresses which all committed Christians would undergo as part of their existence as members of communities of faith. Like nets they, too, would daily require to be restored, strengthened, and made secure for the tasks which must be undertaken.

Today, it is estimated by some statisticians that the Christian church worldwide is daily growing by about 50,000 souls net, allowing for those who depart this life each day. Yet those of us who live in the Western world, apart from in the US, are not used to seeing new converts regularly welcomed into our fellowships in any significant numbers, and there is a longing for the kind of in-gathering, which our forefathers in the faith experienced during times of spiritual revival in the eighteenth and nineteenth centuries, the like of which we have heard of in recent reports from Korea, Kenya, Brazil and Indonesia. Western Christians are often obsessed by problems such as anxiety and depression, and know little of what Hillyer calls 'care-free Christianity'.[6] Yet the latter is exactly what Peter says should be the norm for churches where believers have learned to practise what he preached, and preach what he practised. He is offering us real hope that our current maladies and impasses can be reversed, and that our Christian networks can be mending and mended. And this is not 'pie in the sky when you die' hope. Peter is being realistic when he says that we will all have to suffer 'for a little while' (5:10), in that, as he says in 2 Peter 3:8, 'With the Lord a day is like a thousand years, and a thousand years are like a day.' Struggles are normal throughout Christians' pilgrimage in this world, as resident aliens who are often marginalized, and sometimes persecuted, for their faith, as we saw in chapter 3. But those struggles are time-limited, seasonal, and short by comparison with the eternal glory which awaits God's people in Christ (5:10), and the 'wear and tear' which results can be mended.

In other words, to return to Peter's theme of dealing with difficulties caused by domineering church leaders, we have to make up our minds, as a priority, not to conform any longer to this-worldly patterns of organizational behaviour, and allow God increasingly to transform our attitudes and actions by informing and inspiring us with his mind on the matter. For Paul says that, through the apostolic scriptures, 'We have the mind of Christ' (1 Cor. 2:16), which means that thought and will, as they are related to morality, are informed and inspired by the exalted Lord in the growing experience of those who have received the Spirit of God. Yet Paul, like Peter, was only too aware of the fact that within the churches there are people at various stages of Christian growth: 'I could not address you as spiritual but as worldly – mere infants in Christ . . . For since there is jealousy and quarrelling among you, are you not worldly?' (1 Cor. 3:1-3). That kind of immaturity had led to divisions in the Corinthian church into sycophantic groupings, each favouring their absent heroes Paul, Apollos, or Peter – and others were even claiming to be far superior, as true followers of Christ (1:12; 3:4-23).

The radical realism of the apostles makes us face up to the fact that so often our own congregations have been divided by disputes of one kind and another, and factions have formed which have led to breakdowns in fellowship for a time, or even for generations. In Scotland we know all too much about the kind of divisive behaviour of which Paul speaks openly here, as our Presbyterian churches have often experienced splits and disruptions at various levels, local and national, with a resultant weakening of united Christian witness, within a relatively small nation. The problem is that we have got so used to disunity that we have lost sight of the unifying vision of Christ for his body, the church, and have proudly refused to avail ourselves of the gracious help which God continues to offer: 'The God of all grace . . . will himself restore you and make you strong' (1 Pet. 5:10). This promise of God's ongoing restoration and strengthening of his people is rooted in Peter's earlier quotation of Proverbs 3:34, 'God shows favour to the humble and oppressed' (5:5), which is the source of every solution to the pastoral problems with which Peter is dealing – including authoritarian leadership, or 'lording it' (5:3). In other words, the stresses and strains which are caused by such domineering behaviour need not destroy a fellowship of believers if the congregation as a whole is determined to address the issues: 'All of you, clothe yourselves with humility toward one another' (5:5), says Peter, emphasizing, through the Greek word order, that it should be *all*, as there are always some professing Christians who are quite willing to be 'human doormats', and others who are quite lazy and unwilling to take appropriate responsibility and therefore are happy to let their leaders rule the roost and do the lion's share of the work. Peter is challenging this kind of attitude and offering hope that it is possible for individual congregations and groups of churches to be delivered from domination and discover the true liberty of God's children as members of his household of faith in the midst of a hostile or complacent world which often keeps them at arms' length. Peter emphasizes that God promises increasingly to deliver churches from such internal weaknesses, as well as to protect them from external threats and to equip them for effective and joyful service together.

Mending the mind

How is this 'mending' to be carried out? Peter says that God will do it, but that clearly does not imply that we can do nothing to avail ourselves of his gracious work. Peter's paraenesis exhorts us, together and as individuals, to humble ourselves, to cast our anxieties on God, to be self-controlled and alert, and to resist the devil (1 Pet. 5:6–9). All of these are basically about mental, moral, and spiritual attitudes and actions, including prayer and a positive response to the preaching of the word of God. They are Peter's way of saying what Paul urged the Roman Christians to do:

> Therefore, I urge you, brothers and sisters, in view of God's mercy, to offer your bodies as a living sacrifice, holy and pleasing to God – this is true worship. Do not conform to the pattern of this world, but be transformed by the renewing of your mind. Then you will be able to test and approve what God's will is – his good, pleasing, and perfect will (Rom. 12:1–2).

In fact, Paul then goes on to address the same set of issues upon which Peter has focused in 1 Peter 5:

> Do not think of yourself more highly than you ought . . . in Christ we, though many, form one body, and each member belongs to all the others. We have different gifts, according to the grace given to each of us . . . if it is serving, then serve; if it is teaching, then teach . . . if it is to lead, do it diligently . . . Live in harmony with one another. Do not be proud, but be willing to associate with people of low position. Do not think you are superior' (Rom. 12:3–16).

The kind of transformation that Paul and Peter envisaged for the churches which they served was to result from an ongoing process of mental renewal and spiritual commitment, which has ethical consequences. The mending has to begin with the mind.

Peter states, from the very beginning of this letter, that our minds matter. In 1 Peter 1:13 he again uses language very similar to Paul's in Romans: 'Therefore you people whose minds are girded for action, who are sober, must set your hope totally upon the grace that comes to you at the appearance of Jesus Christ.'[7] Nowadays, we in the Western world have no need to gird up our long robes in order to engage in some arduous activity! In modern parlance, this should be paraphrased, 'Roll up the sleeves of your mind.' Peter realized that if Christians are going to live disciplined and different lives they must be ready for some tough mental work, on a daily basis. The Greek word *dianoia* used for *mind* here is very common in the Septuagint and New Testament, and signifies a mental and volitional capacity which was theirs by virtue of their redemption in Christ, rather than indicating mere natural intellectual powers.[8] It signifies our ability to think, our faculty of knowledge, our understanding, our mind, or the disposition of our will. Peter saw that people's lives are shaped by their thinking, and that their desires and feelings are closely connected with their minds. That's why he says, in 1:14, 'As obedient children, you must not continue to be people shaped by the desires that were characteristic of your former time of ignorance.'[9] In other words, feelings must be in conformity with facts, and not vice versa, for those who want to follow the way of Christian realism. But that does not mean a retreat into reductionism and rationalism. On the contrary, it's another way of treating the ancient biblical theme of loving God with heart, soul and strength (Deut. 6:5).[10] Mark quotes Jesus' use of this Old Testament verse in Mark 12:30 and adds the word *mind*: 'Love the Lord your God with all your heart and with all your soul and with all your mind and with all your strength.' For Peter, the concept of mind was connected with the Hebrew notion of the heart (*lēb*), whereby 'understanding' itself becomes a disposition, an attitude, and thus a standpoint of faith.[11] We believe in order to know – our knowledge and understanding are not just about assent to the truth, but involve our experience of it.

CBT and bibliotherapy

The problem is to find the resources to enable our minds to be open to the mending which the Lord is willing and able to encourage, so that we can recover from the regular stresses and strains of trying to live a Christian life, along with our fellow believers, as resident aliens in occupied territory. In the rest of this chapter we will seek, among other things, to explore the connections which may be constructively made between Cognitive Behavioural Therapy (CBT) and Peter's rhetorical method for changing the behaviour of Christians – his paraenesis.

Cognition is a technical word for thought. We can easily get into patterns of thinking which are not only unbiblical, but which are negative and destructive. We can find ourselves believing things which are simply not true, both about ourselves and about others. The psychiatrist and psychologist David D. Burns, one of the leading specialists in the field of CBT, has analysed the various forms which our twisted thinking may take.[12] B. and G. Passantino define CBT in this way:

> Cognitive-behavioral therapy progresses through several stages: education about the relationship between thoughts and personal well-being, training in assessing one's thoughts and comparing them to external reality, training in how to modify one's thoughts to accurately reflect reality, and, in some applications of cognitive-behavioral therapy, an additional time of learning to translate one's new thought patterns into both a comprehensive world view and correspondingly healthy actions. Several features or goals of some behavioral therapies have been used by Christians in a Christian world view setting, such as assumptions about rational apprehension of reality, and changing behavior to correspond to truth.[13]

Chris Williams, a senior lecturer in Psychiatry in the University of Glasgow, Scotland, has produced a 'Christian self-help approach to depression and anxiety' along with Paul Richards, an experienced Baptist pastor, and a consultant psychiatrist, Ingrid Whitton.[14] This book is the most useful tool currently available for church leaders in the English-speaking world who want to develop skills in pastoral care which can enable them to discern negative thinking patterns in themselves and their people and to plan to engage in preaching and pastoral work with a keen awareness of how church leaders can both promote and discourage healthy thinking and, through that, influence mental health for good or ill. It also provides information about psychiatric approaches to anxiety and depression and the use of drugs. It is not intended as a replacement for professional consultation with psychologists or psychiatrists; in fact, it provides information and insights which could aid the process of referral when pastors recognize that they are getting out of their depth. I recommend this book, as well as that of Burns, wholeheartedly, having benefited personally from them both in addressing negative thought patterns in myself and also in better understanding those who are in my pastoral care.

In his analysis of unhelpful thinking styles Burns uses ten headings, which Williams et al. summarize under six points:[15]

1. I may have a bias against myself, in which I tend to overlook my strengths and accentuate my weaknesses, downplay what I have achieved, and act as my own worst critic.
2. I may have a tendency towards putting a negative slant on things, with my mind filtering out positive thoughts. That may mean seeing only the potentially threatening or harmful in situations.
3. I may entertain a gloomy view of the future and make negative predictions, jumping to conclusions that things are going to work out catastrophically. Not only may I think negatively but believe the worst possible events could happen.
4. I may engage in a kind of mind-reading where I believe I can surely know what others are thinking about me, often assuming that I am not liked or valued by them.
5. I can take responsibility myself for all that goes wrong, believing that I should be able to make things go better for others, and in so doing take unfair responsibility for things that are clearly not my fault, or within my power to change.
6. I may tend towards making extreme statements or rules, whereby I imagine that I am 'always' guilty of certain failings, or that a course of action is 'typical' of my weaknesses, or that I can 'never' get things right. That may also include making up unhelpful rules where I determine in advance what must, should or ought to be.

Such biased and extreme thought patterns are almost always untrue, suggest Williams et. al., leading not only to a drop in mood so that we feel more depressed, upset, anxious, stressed or angry, but also to unhelpful changes in behaviour, including avoidance, reduced activity, or drinking heavily. Williams and his co-authors have produced very helpful worksheets to enable us to work through such issues, as has Burns.

This form of psychotherapy, therefore, is rooted in the belief that our thoughts affect our feelings and vice versa, in a vicious circle of unhelpful behaviours.[16] When, for example, we are depressed or anxious, we tend to think negatively or be filled with dread about certain outcomes. CBT sets about changing the thought patterns of people who are depressed or anxious by exposing those thought patterns and replacing them with more positive, hopeful, and constructive ways for those individuals to think about themselves, their heredity and their environment.

> Part of anxiety and depression is a tendency to judge things in extreme and unhelpful ways that distort how we see ourselves, God, people we know and the events that occur to us. These extreme ways of seeing things are often learned very early on in our lives and such unhelpful thinking tends to worsen when we feel anxious or depressed. Unhelpful thinking often becomes worse when we face difficult situations, relationship or practical problems, particularly when we think that we are trapped and overwhelmed.[17]

A key part of CBT as practised by Burns, Williams and others is what they call bibliotherapy – the use of a prescribed text with exercises for clients to work through between appointments with the therapist, such as Burns's own best-selling book, *The Feeling Good Handbook*, and Williams et al., *I'm not supposed to feel like this*. Burns cites several reasons for the popularity of his book, and refers to research studies which have corroborated his own findings over the years. Several studies have indicated that depressed patients treated with CBT are more likely to improve quickly and to remain free of depression for several years following the initial recovery period.[18] As long ago as the mid-1970s, the first controlled-outcome study of CBT for depression was carried out, in which depressed patients were randomly assigned to one of two treatment groups. Patients in the first group were treated with the drug imipramine, one of the most widely used antidepressants then and now. Those people were treated only with the drug, while the second group received CBT alone. The latter improved as much as, if not more than, the former group. Since then dozens of studies have confirmed that for depressed adults, CBT is at least as good as and perhaps better than antidepressants in dealing with mild to severe depressions. For depressed children and adolescents, the studies concluded that there is little or no evidence that drugs are always effective and that CBT should be used first. In fact, recent studies have shown that the effects of drug treatment tend to wear off after a time, so that the medication becomes less effective. The view that depression is a biological and genetic disorder and that antidepressant drugs should provide the front-line in treatment seems not to be thoroughly grounded in scientific facts, suggests Burns. Of course, the claim that self-help books can be useful is itself controversial, but has also been the subject of academic research. Bibliotherapy can be done in two ways: either to read between therapy sessions, or to read without any psychotherapy or drug treatment. Interestingly, studies have shown that in cases of mild to moderate depression, the exclusive use of a self-help book such as those of Burns and Williams et al. can be as effective as a full course of psychotherapy or treatment with the latest antidepressant drugs. In fact, a wide range of problems besides depression, such as anxiety disorders, interpersonal conflicts such as marriage difficulties, or confrontations in the workplace, have been shown to respond positively to CBT by bibliotherapy. 'The researchers concluded that while a self-help book could have significant antidepressant effects, this would not necessarily be true of any self-help book. The book must contain sound information about how to overcome depression.'[19] Furthermore, more recent studies of severely depressed patients have come to similar conclusions. The use of the self-help book seemed to have substantial and lasting antidepressant effects. The researchers also concluded that bibliotherapy was effective not only for depressed subjects, but might also be effective in public education and in depression prevention programmes. Burns concludes that the research demonstrates the benefits of CBT and bibliotherapy, while recognizing that there is a place for drug treatments and individual and group therapies. He admits that 30 per cent of those in the studies who only read the self-help book did not recover. He has never been opposed to the use of medication, and recognizes that some patients do respond well to drug treatment. But many others do not:

> Certainly they did not return to joyous, productive living when they took these drugs. This is why I spent so much of my career researching and developing new psychological treatments, to have more weapons to fight depression than just drugs . . . These negative thinking patterns can be immensely deceptive and persuasive, and change is rarely easy. But with patience and persistence, I

believe that nearly all individuals suffering from depression can improve and experience a sense of joy and self-esteem once again.[20]

Cross-cultural issues

Recent studies have also indicated that depressive tendencies and low self-esteem can be prevalent in cultures where there are high levels of presentation of various symptoms and attitudes. Carol Craig notes this about her native Scotland:

> Why do the Scots lack confidence in themselves and their country? . . . A strong tendency to criticise and focus on what is wrong with something rather than to praise, appreciate or be positive . . . An overwhelming sense that people's behaviour can be judged right or wrong, worthless or useless . . . A prevailing notion that if any-one makes a mistake or does anything wrong, no excuses will be permitted in their defence and that they should be blamed and criticised for their misdemeanours. An undeveloped sense of pri-vacy: everything you do in life could be the focus of others' criti-cism and censure . . . A general belief that you are not okay just as you are and that you must compete and prove your worth . . . A strong set of egalitarian values which stress that no-one is more important than anyone else and a culture where people are rou-tinely put down if they are seen to get above themselves . . . A pre-vailing belief that it is better if people do not like themselves too much . . . A strong sense that if you question Scottish values or step outside conventional behaviour or opinions your very right to call yourself 'Scottish' may be under threat.[21]

We see from Craig's analysis that the factors pinpointed by propo-nents of CBT may become enculturated. That means that certain cultural cues may actually be a reflection of destructive patterns of thought, which may commonly be understood to be part of the way of life in certain countries or cultures. Scotland has levels of mental ill health which are unenviably high in comparison with other European nations, and it is estimated that 25 per cent of the population will need treatment for psychiatric problems at some time during their lives. Scotland also has the highest suicide rate in the UK. The attitudes which characterize everyday life in Scotland, and to a certain extent among Scots overseas, have once humorously been summarized in the Scots language as, 'Wha's like us? Gie few – an they're a deid!' (Who are like us? Very few, and they're all dead!) The cocky Scot likes to think that there is nowhere like Scotland and nobody like the Scot. She or he values the communitarian ideals which have distinguished Scottish history and thought from those of Scotland's near neighbours, the more individualistic English. Yet, as individuals, the Scots often display a lack of self-assurance and confidence, and mostly downplay their strengths and over-emphasize their weaknesses. We must be careful not to stereotype any people group or population, but Carol Craig's attempt at understanding why we Scots are the way we are is a brave and valuable contribution to the ongoing debate about the distinctive qualities of Scotland and the Scots.

Because of the Scots' crisis of confidence we can understand the attraction of certain movements within the worldwide Christian church which from time to time have an impact on Scotland and her church. A national Kirk which is recognized as the mother church by millions of Presbyterians throughout the world has fallen on hard times. Membership which was 1,233,800 in 1966 had fallen to 504,360 by 2006, of whom only one third were active in worship, fellowship, and service. Yet Scottish Christians exported their way of doing church throughout the British Empire, having stood up to English tyrants in the seventeenth century, through the days of the Covenanters and beyond. Today, we are net importers of religious ideas and programmes, mostly from North America.

It is interesting that the most influential current church renewal system is called The Purpose Driven Church,[22] which originated in California, in Orange County's Saddleback Church, under Baptist pastor Rick Warren. This is the latest in a string of imports, many of which came out of that sun-soaked western state of the USA. Of course, to have purpose is essential to the healthy development of any human group, and churches are not exempt. One of the greatest theologians of the Catholic Church, Augustine of Hippo in North Africa, expressed that overriding sense of purpose in one of the most famous prayers ever penned:

Almighty God, in whom we live and move and have our being, you have made us for yourself and our hearts are restless until they find their rest in you. Grant us purity of heart and strength of purpose, that no selfish passion may hinder us from knowing your will, no weakness from doing it; but that in your light we may see light clearly, and in your service we may find our perfect freedom; through Jesus Christ our Lord.[23]

Augustinian theology was, of course, one of the most important sources for John Calvin and the Reformed tradition. It could be argued that Scottish Christians have historically been very purposeful, and not shy in exporting and promoting a version of Reformed Christianity which has involved systematic indoctrination (through the use of teaching ministries and catechisms, etc.), structured governance (through ministers and elders organized in Kirk Sessions, Presbyteries, and General Assemblies, without the need for bishops), and social action (through the provision of schools in every parish, and the development of health programmes and hospitals). In many ways, the Church of Scotland provided models for democratic ideals, with its rejection of episcopacy and its claim of right that congregations should be able to elect their own ministers and those who represent them in Presbyteries and General Assemblies.

Scottish Reformed theology and Scottish common sense philosophy had a big influence on the thinking of the eighteenth-century founders of the US, who spoke, in their Declaration of Independence (1776), of the 'self-evident' rights of all people to life, liberty, and the pursuit of happiness.[24] Rick Warren also believes that his formula for church renewal is self-evidently and universally applicable, and his first book has sold half a million copies worldwide, having been translated into a number of languages. So we Scots should not be annoyed or embarrassed if some of our historical spiritual investment is returned to our shores, with interest, in the twenty-first century! Yet one can hardly imagine any two places that are more different – geographically, culturally and psychologically – than the California and Scotland of today. Warren describes his feat of planting a church from scratch near to the booming computer industries of Silicon Valley, and admits that most of the people in his church are well-heeled and well-educated with high expectations of what church can do for them and their families, and of what they can do for their church. Warren does constantly refer to the phenomenal growth of his congregation, from zero to over 10,000, over a period of fifteen years, because many Americans highly value success and growth, and the 'megachurch' is attractive to them as a concept. People are willing to travel long distances to participate, and their parking lot is breathtakingly large!

Self-evident success?

And Warren is not alone in his self-confident advocacy of his own systems, believing that the pattern of his ministry and the experience of his congregation should be transferable cross-culturally, both within his homeland and internationally. During the 1990s management guru Stephen Covey, as noted above, was developing management and leadership systems which have been exported worldwide. He, too, believes that the principles upon which he bases his approach are 'self-evident' and universalizable.

This is not a new phenomenon, but part of the issue of cross-cultural communication, a discipline within social and cultural anthropology. Missiology is concerned largely with this issue, but the need to appreciate the nuances of cross-cultural communication is often lost on those who seek to communicate within a language group, as in the English-speaking world. While a Californian, for example, will spend years preparing to work as a mission partner and learning the language and culture of non-English speakers, one wonders whether those who export their Christian subcultural norms from the US have worked as hard at bridging the cultural gap between, for example, America and Scotland. Just because we speak roughly the same language, that does not mean that we are immediately able to understand and appreciate the cultural nuances and assumptions which communication involves. And we are unlikely to try and understand those of others if we simply believe and assert that our own are self-evident and universalizable, assertions which may be justified in philosophical or political discourse, but which are inappropriate in theological discussion.

The whole idea that one's concepts about management or any other human activity are 'self-evidently' valid is open to criticism at a number of levels. It is understandable that Americans who appreciate the traditions enshrined in their constitutional documents should imagine that their ideals should be universally valued and shared. The recent war in Iraq, for example, was waged in order to effect a regime change in Baghdad and to open the way for Western-style democracy. As I write, Iraq is embroiled in a civil war between Sunni and Shia Muslims, as well as in insurgency against the occupation forces of the US and UK. The dream of democracy seems light years away from the harsh realities which are faced every day on the streets of that beleaguered nation. There was much talk, when the initial invasion was effected, of 'winning the hearts and minds of the Iraqi people'. However, as Lingenfelter and Mayers have shown, their fellow Americans are often shocked when they try to take their assumptions into other cultural situations, both within the US and overseas. 'Culture is the conceptual design, the definitions by which people order their lives, interpret their experience, and evaluate the behaviour of others.'[25]

Learning to communicate cross-culturally is essentially about enculturation, by which an individual acquires the cultural heritage of a larger community, and involves a process of conflict, questioning, and acceptance. Wherever we live, we share certain beliefs and values and a way of life with many other people around us. In order to be effective Christian communicators within a culture which is new to us, 'We are to become incarnate in the cultures to which we are sent.'[26] This reflects the theological position of the apostle Paul in his seminal missiological statement:

> Though I am free and belong to no one, I have made myself a slave to everyone, to win as many as possible. To the Jews I became like a Jew, to win the Jews. To those under the law I became like one under the law (though I myself am not under the law), so as to win those under the law. To those not having the law I became like one not having the law (though I am not free from God's law but am under Christ's law), so as to win those not having the law. To the weak I became weak, to win the weak. I have become all things to all people so that by all possible means I might save some. I do all

this for the sake of the gospel, that I may share in its blessings (1 Cor. 9:19–23).

This missiological goal has specific implications for the way people organize themselves and communicate with one another and with those beyond the bounds of their culture.

In order to enable their readers to gain expertise in cross-cultural communication, Lingenfelter and Mayers isolate ten primary message systems which obtain in every culture:

1. Language; 2. Temporality (time, routine, schedule); 3. Territoriality (space, property); 4. Exploitation (methods of control – use and sharing of resources); 5. Association (family, kinship, community); 6. Subsistence (work, division of labour); 7. Bisexuality (different modes of speech, dress, conduct); 8. Learning (observation, modelling, instruction); 9. Play (humor, games); 10. Defence (health procedures, social conflicts, beliefs). Each message system has its rules governing relationships and communication; each has its structure, pattern, and variations which must be learned. One might conclude by this very crude measure that knowing a language opens up only about one-tenth of what one could learn about a total lifestyle, a culture.[27]

As we explore these layers, we recognize how easy it is to focus on 1. while ignoring 2. to 9. British imperialists took the English language around the world, but also exported values enshrined in the other nine points of contact. We made the same kind of mistakes as some of our American cousins may now be repeating, so we are in no position to pretend that we are faultless in this whole area. There seems to be something inherent in human nature which tends to make us believe that our own worldview is superior to that of others, and self-evidently so. However, with the advance of globalization we really do need to ensure that we do not view the needs and aspirations of the worldwide church through the eyes of the current high-achievers in terms of popular programmes and numerical church growth. To be highly effective is a value which is implicit in contemporary Western societies, but how is that effectiveness to be measured? I would suggest that there are some who focus on quantity and others who prefer quality. That would be true of various traditions even within the English-speaking world alone. So it is very dangerous to attempt the project which Rick Warren and others seem to be determined to develop if the number of translations of his books is any gauge of their visions.

If the worldwide church comprises mending networks, then twenty-first-century Christians must learn the postmodern skills of holistic and synthetic thinking, which seek to bring together the issues raised in this chapter. That means moving away from notions such as 'self-evident', and embracing understandings of knowing which take into account the standpoint of the reader of any text. Warren and Covey assume that their readers, all over the world, will accept their assertions that everybody should almost automatically see that their main points are just common sense, and valid no matter where on earth their readers live. That implies that Western Christian networks have no need to be mending or to be mended, and that our ways of thinking should be universally adopted, which rules out genuine dialogue and understanding. In fact, it confirms the postmodern suspicion that big stories which seek to offer grand explanations of human history and society are written by the winners, those who imagine that life can be win-win for all participants. Christian leaders have, however, for centuries sought, however poorly, to imitate Christ, whose story is not win-win, but lose-win. They have engaged in pastoral ministry in the dynamic of the death and resurrection of Christ, as Peter and the other apostles did in the beginning. So, in our final two chapters we must try to make sense of this tradition, and see how scriptural resources may validly be used in order to promote pastoral formation and deal with aspects of the ministry of Christian leaders which may, for various reasons, become misleading and distorted. Instead of writing another self-help manual, this author now seeks to produce a Scripture help guide for prospective leaders, those already in pastoral ministry, and others who want to support and promote excellence in church leadership in the twenty-first century. The success or failure of that project is about two-way traffic. Will you join me?

Summary

Let's summarize where this chapter has taken us:

- Mending nets was good training for developing Christian mending networks in the early church and beyond. Peter's paraenesis is based on the practicalities of teamworking.
- Mending the church begins with the mind. Peter says, 'Roll up the sleeves of your mind!'
- Christian leaders are called to work with God, who restores and strengthens his people.
- Resources for restoration can be found in non-selfist therapies such as Cognitive Behavioural Therapy (CBT) as well as in pastoral theologies, rather than in selfist psychologies.
- Care must be taken when attempting to export church growth and development methodologies cross-culturally, especially within language groups such as English.
- We must beware of claims that certain approaches and strategies are self-evidently valid within the multifarious expressions of the universal church.

9

Leading Habits and Purpose

Cultural commentators believe that many twenty-first-century Americans, and not a few Europeans, are in search of the one lifestyle programme that will do it all. Many are striving to reduce their weight, while eating all they want, and trim and tone their bodies, with no more than ten minutes of exercise per day. Many want a self-confident and pushy personality that others cannot resist and to learn the secrets of being a success in every area of life – business, DIY, sport, relationships, church, etc. – by simply listening to a tape or reading a self-help book. What is the attraction of today's lifestyle gurus? They promise significance, success, wealth, fame, efficiency, wholeness, balance, integration, promotion, peace of mind, long life and endless fulfilment. And millions believe they can deliver it. The sale of their products and publications that promise all this and more has grown into a multimillion dollar industry, with some of their authors and instructors gaining 'talk-show' celebrity status, ensuring that their books and videos become best-sellers. A number of such books have been translated into several languages.

Covey's 'seven habits' today

One of the most popular training manuals in this genre is, of course, Stephen Covey's *The 7 Habits of Highly Effective People* and its various spin-off books and programmes, such as *The 7 Habits of Highly Effective Families*. Covey's organization, the Franklin Covey Company, claims at this time to have over 19,000 licensed facilitators teaching its curriculum to over 750,000 participants every year. These include 82 of the American Fortune 100 companies (similar to Britain's FT 100 Index), thousands of small- and medium-sized companies, government bodies, educational institutions, communities, families, and millions of individual consumers. Annual book sales are reported to be over 1.5 million, with over 15 million individuals using the organization's life planner products. Among these participants and book purchasers are Christians, including business executives, pastors and denominational leaders.

While some of the principles in *The 7 Habits (SH)* are clearly beneficial and contain some applications that will work in many situations, should this book have a prominent place in the Christian home and church? Are there any problems that we as contemporary Christians might justifiably have concerning this material?[1]

To understand the *SH* model we need to be aware of the author's philosophical and theological presuppositions. Stephen Covey is a devout, practising member of the Church of Jesus Christ of Latter-day Saints (LDS), or Mormon Church, and has written not only personal development books marketed through secular bookstores, but also books intended for a Mormon market. He has served the LDS Church in a number of positions, including as full-time missionary and as bishop, and on several Mormon leadership and teacher development committees. His book, *The Divine Center (DC)*, is about centring one's life in the god of Mormonism and reads like a LDS primer. In fact, *DC* seems to be the basis for *SH*, as many of the ideas that Covey expounds in it are included and developed in *SH*. So *SH* is the author's way of conveying ideas previously presented to Mormons in *DC* to a non-LDS audience. He advises fellow Mormons, '. . . we shouldn't hesitate to work within the vocabularies of others to communicate our meanings . . . we can teach and testify of many gospel principles if we are careful in selecting words which carry our meaning but come from their experience and frame of mind'.[2] This blurring of distinctions is a common ploy used by LDS leaders in engaging with non-Mormons, particularly orthodox Christians. In *SH* Covey claims these are self-evident and universal principles, not 'unique to any specific faith or religion, including my own. These principles are a part of most every major enduring religion as well as social philosophies and ethical systems'. 'The more closely our maps or paradigms are aligned with these principles or natural laws, the more accurate and functional they will be.'[3]

Catholic, ecumenical and evangelical Christians are not immune to Covey's theories, which many find to be convincing. After all, many of us are wondering how on earth we can fit everything in to our increasingly busy lives – with sufficient time for the family, friends and the church – while achieving our goals, coping with demands at work, answering the emails, pleasing the boss, having a successful marriage, raising perfect children, getting enough exercise, detoxing the body, etc.

Covey claims that effective people are those who do not lose sight of the bigger things in life, who manage their diaries to ensure that however busy and demanding each day is, the important things are never neglected. They are people who develop habits which enable them to achieve everything they want effectively and smoothly. They are people who routinely monitor their success, with a view to constant improvement. They are focused individuals who will get to the end of their lives and look back with satisfaction at all they have achieved. At least that is the claim of Covey and his teams. But what can we say in response to such self-evident self-assurance?

Covey says a lot about the importance of character and having a principled value system, but he leaves it open to his readers to import whatever goals or values they prefer. So at the end of the day, although apparently attractive, his route to self-perfection is deeply flawed. It relies, like other secular alternatives, on a self-orientated attempt to fulfilment and a self-centred definition of success. It has been particularly attractive to people in leadership positions, both secular and ecclesiastical. How does this square with the leading habits which Peter set about encouraging in his letters?

We have discovered in this book that 1 Peter was written to churches scattered across the eastern Roman Empire, in Asia Minor. They were under pressure, living in a hostile, anti-Christian, secular yet sacralized world, where they were marginalized as resident aliens. Christian leaders were increasingly under pressure to conform to the status quo of imperialist paternalistic leadership styles, and they were challenged by Peter not to lord it over the congregations of the faithful, but to provide examples for others to follow, as they themselves sought to follow Peter, and through him and his associates to learn to follow Christ. We can see the relevance of Peter's teaching to our own context in the UK of today. The London Institute for Contemporary Christianity recently brought together representatives from a large number of Christian organizations concerned about the ways in which British society and its judicial systems are increasingly hostile to religious freedom of expression and, in particular, the right to share faith in public or speak of Jesus as the Son of God and Lord of all. They pointed out that just as in the first century, Christians today are losing their jobs, being arrested, fined and even face going to prison for being obedient to Jesus Christ in the UK.[4] For example, the Roman Catholic goalkeeper of Glasgow Celtic football club was recently cautioned by the police for crossing himself on the field of play! In January 2006 Mario Conti, the Roman Catholic Archbishop of Glasgow, said in a sermon that the moral teaching of the church was being undermined due to the Scottish Parliament's decision to enable same-sex couples to form civil partnerships recognized by the state. He complained that this new legislation 'weakens the uniqueness of marriage as a time-honoured, legally recognized and protected social reality and a fiscally privileged entity. It also implicitly places homosexual acts on a plane of moral equivalence to marital love.'[5] In reaction to this a member of the Scottish Parliament wrote to the Chief Constable of Strathclyde Police asking him to investigate Conti's remarks, believing them to be homophobic. Christian leaders who maintain orthodox traditions are under pressure today, as in Peter's time. The latest instance of this in the UK is the insistence by government, in new legislation which seeks to enshrine the principles of the European Charter of Human Rights, that there should be no exceptions to the rule that same-sex couples should be free from discrimination in the process of adoption. Roman Catholic adoption agencies have asked to be exempted, with the support of the Anglican Archbishops of Canterbury and York.

What, then, are the leading habits which Peter promotes through his circular letter to the churches, 1 Peter, and how may they be understood and applied in today's Western church and world? In addition, how do they compare with the priorities established in Rick Warren's model of church organization and leadership, with its claim to be 'purpose driven'? Of course, the concept of habit in the New Testament is rooted in the word 'ethos', meaning 'custom', 'usage',[6] from which we derive the English word ethics. This is rooted in the Septuagint, where *ethos* conveys the idea of basic human motives or attitudes, a frame of mind, or a way of life which results from certain ethical or psychological impulses. It reflects the idea that, in any culture, there are certain customary dispositions and ways of behaving, whether in connection with religious practices, popular morality, or personal habits. To seek to understand those habits, which Peter proposes as effective for existing or potential Christian leaders, is to explore Peter's ethical exhortation, his paraenesis, which has been the focus of much of our discussion in this book. In this chapter we must   gather those themes which particularly connect with the habits of leading, then and now. Our interest in Warren's work will also enable us to understand what the nature of purpose is in New Testament thinking and pastoral theology and to help us discern those aspects which transcend cultural distinctives.

Peter and prayer

For Peter, the clash of customs was a very significant context of his apostolic ministry as described by Luke in Acts. In fact, scholars are agreed that the various speeches and strategies which are described are chosen because they are typical of the apostolic missions.[7] The notes of Peter's sermons and interaction with key people are presented to give the reader a clear idea as to his customary approaches to communication and caring. In other words, Luke shows us more than is overtly described, and gives us summaries, even of encounters which appear to be strategic new directions for the churches. We see from the first gatherings of the infant church, recorded in Acts 1:14, that one of the habits which Peter practised was that of prayer with the community of faith, a group of some 120 following the ascension of Christ. But there is more. Peter, the male disciples and the apostles regularly prayed with the women, which represented a radical, even revolutionary, change. In the synagogue, men and women were separated and never joined in prayer. Praying with women was not the only new habit which Peter fostered in those early days, which reflected his willingness to change old habits.

Peter and his Jewish past

Following his encounter with God through a vision and visit from the centurion Cornelius in Acts 10, Peter had to manage change in a very skilful way, culminating in the Council of Jerusalem in Acts 15. Stephen (Acts 6:14) and Paul (26:3) were both accused of changing the customs delivered by Moses. Peter's memoirs of Jesus' ministry as recorded by Mark also include awareness of controversy over customs which were really ethical questions. The Pharisees complained to Jesus, 'Look, why are they [the disciples] doing what is unlawful [picking ears of grain] on the Sabbath?' (Mk. 2:24). Jesus dealt with that using casuistry, or a case study, rather than trying to justify his position from a particular part of the Law of Moses. He chose the story of David's decision to let his men eat bread which had previously been offered to God, despite the fact that the Law said that only priests should partake. Jesus concluded, 'The Sabbath was made for people; not people for the Sabbath' (Mk. 2:27). Here is a habit for every Christian leader to aspire to: the interpretation and application of Scripture as far as possible with God's original gracious intention in mind, rather than the accrued misunderstandings reflected in traditions which serve only to empower certain interest groups rather than promote the good of the whole church. The leading espoused by Peter involves the courage to break free from such stultifying influences, and to make a habit of it. Then, in Mark 3:2ff, Jesus was in the synagogue and his accusers were there watching if he would heal anybody on the Sabbath. They were speechless when Jesus asked them, 'Which is lawful on the Sabbath? To do good or to do evil? To save life or to kill?' Again, in 7:14f, Jesus deals with the issue of ritual uncleanness, and shows that he is in the process of changing Jewish customs for ever: 'Listen to me, everyone, and understand this. Nothing outside you can defile you by going into you. Rather it is what comes

out of you that defiles you.' Peter understood what Jesus was
doing, as noted in parenthesis in v. 19: '(In saying this, Jesus
declared that all foods are clean.)'.

Now the amazing thing is that despite this clear teaching,
Peter took many years to follow Jesus faithfully regarding this
issue. It was only after his vision, recorded in Acts 10:9–23, that
he implemented Christ's declaration that all foods are fit to eat.
In his dream Peter struggled with the Lord's command to kill
and eat all kinds of animals, reptiles and birds. 'Surely not, Lord!
I have never eaten anything impure or unclean' (10:14). Three
times he was commanded and three times he resisted. The house
in Joppa where he was staying was owned by Simon the Tanner,
whose daily work with animal skins meant that he was banned
from synagogue worship. Peter was eating at his table, so the
issue of food laws was not just theoretical for him. Then servants
arrived from the Roman centurion Cornelius, an adherent of the
Jewish synagogue in Caesarea, who had experienced an angelic
appearance and was told to send for Peter. When Peter met
Cornelius and heard of the marvellous providence which had
brought them together, at last the significance of this series of
events dawned on the apostle. 'I now realize how true it is that
God does not show favouritism but accepts those from every
nation who fear him and do what is right' (Acts 10:34). He then
preached the gospel to the Gentile company present, and the
Holy Spirit was poured out on them all. Peter concluded,
'Everyone who believes in him receives forgiveness of sins
through his name' (10:43).

Peter, God's grace and obedience

The news soon reached the church leaders in Jerusalem that the
Gentiles had received the word of God, and Peter was criticized
by Jewish believers for eating with the uncircumcised. Peter told
them of the remarkable happenings which had demonstrated
once and for all that God was doing a new thing. 'So if God gave
them the same gift as he gave us, who believed in the Lord Jesus
Christ, who was I to think that I could stand in God's way?'
(11:17). The response was that they had no further objections,

saying, 'So then, even to Gentiles God has granted repentance that leads to life' (11:18).

Peter had, reluctantly, learned that leading the church meant cultivating the habits of grateful obedience and openness to the grace of God. His privileged position was as one of the eyewitnesses whom God had chosen as apostles, who ate and drank with Jesus after the resurrection and had been personally commissioned to go out into the world with the message. That meant that he would be a recipient of fresh revelation from the exalted Lord, as promised at the Last Supper (Jn. 17:6–19).

When the time came for the Council of Jerusalem, Peter had to deal with the same issues all over again. The Judaizers were coming down from Jerusalem to Antioch in Syria, which had become the base for the Gentile mission, saying that Gentile converts had to be circumcised. By this time, Paul and Barnabas had become established in the Gentile mission, so they went up to meet with James, Peter and the other leaders in Jerusalem. This is the first time that the leadership is specified as the apostles and elders, which shows that the developments we dealt with in chapter 3 were now in place. Peter knew how to deal with the issue, and after much discussion he addressed them, reminding all of what had happened when the Gentiles began to respond to the message of God's kingdom and had received the Holy Spirit, just as at the beginning on the Day of Pentecost. God had made no distinction between Jew and Gentile, so why were they testing God by making demands of Gentiles which the Jews themselves had been unable to bear? Peter said, 'No! We believe it is through the grace of our Lord Jesus that we are saved, just as they are' (15:11). This shows us that the next habit which Peter had acquired was the primacy of grace in his preaching. He didn't mind repeating what he had said earlier, and invited Paul and Barnabas to share stories of what God was doing in the Gentile mission. This was all in response to God's gracious initiative, and James spoke up to register his agreement: 'It is my judgment that we should not make it difficult for the Gentiles who are turning to God' (15:19), he said, having quoted from the prophets who had looked for the time when the God of Israel would be worshipped throughout the world.

Peter's team-playing/team-leading

The interesting thing is that, having made his point, Peter then is happy to act along with the other apostles and elders. The next habit we note is that Peter is a team player who believes in and practises corporate leadership. Despite his tendency during the ministry of Jesus to launch into personal statements and opinions without apparently consulting the others, Peter has now learned that his calling is not to be a monarchical bishop or archbishop, let alone a pope. There is no hint of any self-awareness that Peter is the unique 'rock' of the church, and set apart from the other foundational apostles, as later Catholics claimed. In fact, he is quite happy for James to act as chair of the Jerusalem leadership team at this point.

This is a habit which clearly continued and developed, as by the time Peter writes from Rome the letter that we call 1 Peter, he is content to act with Silas and Mark, as members of an apostolic team, and to acknowledge their part in the composition and propagation of the message. In fact, the account of the Council of Jerusalem is the last word we hear from Peter in the Acts of the Apostles, and Paul takes over as the hero of the remainder of the book. We know nothing for sure about Peter's missionary travels in Asia Minor and his journey to Rome, while we have detailed reports of Paul's itinerary. Yet the one habit which, as we have seen, Peter made his own, quite distinct from Paul's largely mis-siological and theological approach, is his emphasis on paraen-etic preaching, or ethical exhortation. We have seen that Peter adapted the tradition of rhetorical persuasion which was taught by the Greeks, and was unafraid to use categorical imperatives in his writing and proclamation. He was committed to changing the ethos of his hearers, and to help them to develop principles of conduct by which to live their lives and lead the church.

And what of Peter's sense of corporate purpose as an important aspect of his approach to team leadership? Quite rightly, Rick Warren has focused on this aspect of the motivation of the early church as an important rhetorical device. He recognizes that Christians today need to learn disciplined lifestyles and that the churches need to recover the true meaning and purpose of their existence. Above all, twenty-first-century Western Christians are being called to recover a true sense of calling to mission together. As we have seen in earlier chapters, this is no easy task, given the current state of the Western churches and the tendency to think that, if the churches are to grow again, we must seek to provide different kinds of church for many different needs and tastes, or we should aim for a megachurch which is organized like a big business with current management theories as the tools which will guarantee effectiveness. However, such trends overlook one fundamental point which has emerged from our discussion of Peter's paraenetic approach. The rhetorical skills which Peter encourages Christian leaders to adopt are rooted in a Christian ethical vision of the church as a caring family rather than as some multinational corporation.[8] Some of the nuances which he employs are connected with his experience as a businessman, it is true, as we have seen. But his fishing partnership in Galilee was a family business, shared with brother Andrew and the family of Zebedee, his sons James and John. So Peter understood the quite different motivational skills which are required to manage and team-lead the family of God. Three times the risen Lord commanded him to 'Feed/take care of my lambs/sheep' (Jn. 21:16, 17), and then predicted that his death would glorify God, simply calling Peter to 'Follow me!' (21:19). In essence, Peter's model of Christian team-leading was to be counter-cultural and sacrificial.

Our problem today is that our Western culture has been so flooded with self-help books promising the answers to how to be effective and purposeful individuals that we often have taken them on board uncritically without looking more closely at the New Testament to see if our foundational documents contain what we are looking for.[9] This book is seeking to persuade Western Christians that we need look no further than the radical and revolutionary message of the apostles of Jesus Christ, those foundation stones of faith, for true effectiveness and purposefulness in developing leadership in the churches.

In fact, Peter's first recorded sermon, preached at Pentecost, focused on God's purpose: 'People of Israel, listen to this: Jesus of Nazareth was a man accredited by God to you by miracles, wonders and signs, which God did among you through him, as you yourselves know. This man was handed over to you by God's deliberate plan (*boulē*) and foreknowledge; and you, with the help of wicked men, put him to death by nailing him to the cross. But God raised him from the dead' (Acts 2:22–24). Here the Greek word *boulē* is used for 'plan', and is often translated 'purpose'. This reflects Peter's (and Luke's) knowledge of the Septuagint version of the Old Testament. We have argued that Peter would have been fluent in everyday Greek to conduct his business, as well as in Aramaic, and seems to have had a knowledge of key texts in the Septuagint, where *boulē*, meaning 'will', 'resolve' or 'purpose', is used over a hundred times. As we have noted, Peter was influenced greatly by the teaching of Deuteronomy, where we find in 32:28 ('They are a nation without sense, there is no discernment in them') the use of this Greek word to denote 'the weighty consideration which precedes the effecting of the will'.[10] The concern of the Deuteronomist was that the people of Israel historically lacked this wisdom and therefore were making decisions on ephemeral plans and shifting grounds.[11] It was their calling, and that of the church in due course, to reflect God's sense of purpose in all his dealings and determinations. Again and again, believers are caught short in terms of their resolve and willpower to see things through in radical obedience to their God. This is the root meaning of *boulē*, 'purpose', in the Septuagint, which Peter clearly understood and adopted. 'The Lord is not slow in keeping his promise, as some count slowness. He is patient with you, not **purposing** any to perish, but everyone to come to repentance' (2 Pet. 3:9, my translation). Here the verb *boulomai* is used for 'purposing', denoting conscious volition following definite reflection; a decision of the will which presupposes the possibility of freedom of decision. In this case it refers to God's purposing, but it also denotes human volition. Paul uses the verb to indicate an apostolic demand ('I will . . .', 1 Tim. 2:8; 5:14), and James 4:4 uses it of a person who resolves to be a friend of the world. Human purpose can also involve the volitional impulses which may be concealed in the innermost depths of the psyche, of which people may not be conscious (e.g. 1 Cor. 4:5: 'the Lord will expose the motives of people's hearts'). Here it designates a wish determined by personal inclinations, and may stress the will as mental direction and therefore to be translated as intent or intention. It speaks of one's determination to see a plan through to its fruition.[12]

Through 1 Peter, then, the apostle was clearly determined to effect the changing of his hearers' intentions, imaginations and desires, so that they might be people with a purpose. This means rejoicing in sufferings (1:6), thus proving one's faith to be real (1:7), and demonstrating one's love for Christ (1:8). A purposeful faith sets its sights on continued growth in the experience of salvation (1:9). It also involves having prepared minds and set hopes (1:13), while not conforming to evil (1:14). It involves accepting one's lot as a resident alien (1:17) and learning to love other believers profoundly (1:22). At the same time, purposeful Christians set about the task of getting rid of negative attitudes and actions, like malice, deceit and others. They want to grow up in the faith (2:1–3) and to live declaring their praise to God, while abstaining from sinful desires (2:9–11). That means living exemplary lives (2:12) and submission to proper authority (2:13). It means following Christ's example of unjust suffering (2:21ff) and a readiness to give account of the reason for one's faith (3:15). Above all, it is to decide to make God's will our will (3:17, 4:17–19), with the conclusion, 'As a result, they do not live the rest of their earthly lives for evil human desires, but rather for the will of God' (4:2).

Peter's paraenesis and sacrifice

Peter's purposeful people were shown, in this way, that their struggles were at the heart of their calling, and not an unfortunate add-on. God's purpose for them included the grace to sustain them through many trials and tribulations, without which the genuine nature of their faith could not be adequately demonstrated. This was particularly true of those who had been called to lead the church.

It is this kind of thinking which sits very uneasily with some of the latter-day leadership manuals. Think again of Covey's main points: Be Proactive . . . Begin with the End in Mind . . . Put First Things First . . . Think Win-Win . . . Seek First to Understand, then to be Understood . . . Synergize . . . Sharpen the Saw. He believes these seven principles to be 'self-evident, universal and timeless'.[13] But were they all apparent to the leaders whom Peter prepared through his first-century writings? For Covey, being proactive is more than taking the initiative – it involves accepting responsibility for one's own behaviour (past, present, and future) and making decisions based on values and principles rather than on feelings or situations. Peter certainly trained his people to do that, but, unlike Covey, did not leave it open to them which principles they should choose. His ethical exhortation, as we have seen, provides that framework. We must begin, Covey asserts, by creating a mental vision and purpose for any project, resulting in a mission statement. But is that always possible for the church leader? Are there not times when we are unable to see the way ahead so clearly, especially in the kind of hard times which Peter describes? Is it not, then, that human purposefulness is most aptly expressed in prayerfully submitting to the will of God, however hard that may be? Might that, far from being a win-win situation, prove to be lose-lose, win-lose, or lose-win? What does it mean for the believer to live in the rhythm of death and resurrection? That may not be a thought which many American Christians, and others in the wealthy West, might like to dwell upon. But I think of some of the contexts about which David Aikman writes in *Jesus in Beijing* as he relates the story of the contemporary Chinese church.[14] One wonders whether one is not more likely to learn from those whose experience reflects the struggles which Peter clearly expected to be the norm for the churches he addressed, rather than from the cult of so-called success.

Covey believes that 'Creating a culture behind a shared mission, vision, and values is the essence of leadership.'[15] Again, that kind of approach is essential to Peter's paraenesis. Yet it does not always mean that Christian leaders see the end from the beginning. Far from it. Then Covey's 'habits' involve focusing on what matters most for us as individuals and organizations. 'The main thing is to keep the main thing the main thing,' says Covey.[16] Certainly every good leader knows the value of planning and prioritizing, but Christian mission is far more complex even than modern business organization, because the work of God always involves volunteers far more than paid employees, and, therefore, includes those who are at various stages of development and usefulness, as well as many who are on the fringes yet demanding considerable attention from pastoral workers. There are no training programmes that can enable leaders to understand all the dynamics of Christian churches, which are by nature organic rather than organizational in their interrelationships.

Win-Win thinking, for Covey, is not thinking selfishly or like a victim, but interdependently, in terms of 'We not Me'. 'It's sharing information, power, recognition, and rewards.'[17] But is Win-Win the reality most of us aim for day by day? Effectiveness lies in getting the right balance between kindly seeking to understand and courageously seeking to be understood, says Covey. This encourages a synergy, or creative co-operation, which is a third way to 'yours' or 'mine'.

Finally, the metaphor of saw-sharpening is about ongoing renewal in the four basic areas of life: physical, social/emotional, mental and spiritual. Certainly, the wisdom of following the prayer of St Francis, about seeking first to understand and only then to be understood, is an approach which has stood the test of time, as is the call to synergize, to seek to work creatively with others and to act as a good team player, which Peter models for us.

As we come to our tenth and final chapter, we do so having sought to build bridges between current organizational and management thinking and the Christian theology of leading as espoused by the apostles, in particular Peter's insights into leading the church. We must never forget that the word leading is a verbal construct which speaks primarily of action taken rather than of characteristics adopted. The latter might be the focus if we used the noun leadership. It is the job of leaders to lead, in other words, rather than merely to take on board various styles or behaviours. And for leaders to lead effectively, there must be those who are willing to be led. The writer to the Hebrews understood this, and he or she was probably well known to Peter, and part of an apostolic team. 'Remember your leaders, who spoke the word of God to you. Consider the outcome of their way of life and imitate their faith. Jesus Christ is the same yesterday, and today, and forever . . . Have confidence in your leaders and submit to their authority because they keep watch over you as those who must give an account. Do this so that their work will be a joy, not a burden, for that would be of no benefit to you' (Heb. 13:7–8,17).

Summary

In this chapter we have noted Peter's purposeful seven leading habits:

- Prayer in community with both male and female believers.
- Breaking away from dead traditions which had been declared so by Jesus Christ.
- Grateful active obedience to God, learned through ongoing struggle.
- Openness to God's grace, having been given several 'second chances'.
- Primacy of grace in preaching, offering freely what he had freely received.
- Team-playing/team-leading, rather than any thought of rule by apostolic/episcopal succession.
- Ethical exhortation (paraenesis) which is counter-cultural and based on a sacrificial lifestyle.

10

Leading Examples Look East – Peter's Paradigm

As a minister of a Reformed church I am used to the Pauline paradigm[1] for theology and mission. By Pauline paradigm I mean a set of exemplary understandings, standards and expectations which relate to the apostle Paul's significance as a model of Christian discipleship, church planting and development, and as a communicator of reflections on what God is doing in Christ for the church and for the world. But, as Ellis observes, 1 Corinthians, written in 56 CE, 'presents Peter along with Apollos as Paul's fellow apostle and co-worker and as a paradigm with which Paul's apostolic rights may be compared (9:5)'.[2] The late David Bosch, a South African missiologist whose work is widely regarded as seminal for twenty-first-century missional churches, followed the theologian Hans Kung's use of the idea of paradigm shift, which Kung had adapted from the earlier work of the philosopher of science Thomas Kuhn. Bosch suggested that while we may accept Kung's view that there are six definable periods in the history of missions, which can be explained by changing, or shifting, paradigms, it is also true that churches can revisit paradigms and adopt aspects of them as models of orthodoxy and orthopraxis.[3] Since the Reformation, Reformed churches such as those within the Lutheran, Anglican and Presbyterian traditions have returned again and again to the letter to the Romans, believing it to be the fullest statement of the Pauline paradigm, stating clearly Paul's indicatives and imperatives. However, as we have noted, in the process we have tended to underplay other paradigms which may be gleaned from our study of the New

Testament, notably that of Peter. We have recognized that the reasons for this are partly the schisms in the church, which were rooted in claims linking the Roman papacy with Peter's alleged supremacy among the apostles and which Orthodox and Reformed Christians rejected, and partly because of the penchant of some modern scholars for asserting that Peter was not the author of the two letters which bear his name. It is also true that much greater attention has been paid to the missionary methods of Paul, given his prominence in the Acts of the Apostles, and his thirteen extant epistles.[4] We have argued that Peter has something distinctive to contribute to questions concerning patterns of leadership and the proper motivation of Christians for mission and service. Perhaps it is time for another paradigm shift.

Reading 1 Peter today

In this final chapter we must gather the threads of what has been a wide-ranging discussion. Today it is relatively unusual for an author to take the view that one should set about trying to connect first-century organizational patterns with current thinking on management and leadership, as we have sought to do.[5] In the same way, our attempt at linking contemporary psychological theories and therapies with pastoral and missional strategies implicit in New Testament writings may also have appeared strange to some. However, I believe that this kind of approach is validated by Bosch and others, who suggest that the postmodern paradigm currently under development, which emphasizes synthetic rather than analytic thinking,[6] can constructively bring together many strange bedfellows.

For example, in our discussion of motivation in chapter 3 we stressed that it is important to a sense of Christian identity, and in keeping faith alive, through the transformation of conviction and commitment in a world where we are constantly under pressure to conform. We accept that ethical exhortation has been unpopular in twentieth-century Western Protestant churches, and that evangelical Christians have been particularly weak when it comes to understanding and applying ethical principles and moral stances. Yet this remains the chief means of God in empowering people to act both individually and in community in a Christian way. Such motivation is the number one priority for Christian leaders, and our exploration of Peter's first letter in its social context has shown us how his teaching conflicted with the current civil and religious patterns of leadership in Asia Minor. Yet we have established that his hearers were resident aliens, as Abraham had been in his nomadic existence, and as had also the Jewish exiles in Babylon.

Today there are very many believers who live alienated lifestyles yet aspire to serve God in the world. Recently I watched a television report about child labour in the Congo's copper and cobalt mines. It told the harrowing story of three boys who walked two hours six days per week to work, for the wage of 50p each daily, and did not attend school. Yet when asked what their ambitions were, they said they wanted to get an education, and two stated that they hoped to become Christian pastors. They have been touched by the amazing contemporary growth of the churches in Africa south of the Sahara. Yet their brothers and sisters in the wealthy West are doing little or nothing to relieve their abject poverty and the daily injustices which they face. How will they read the first letter of Peter when they have learned to read? Will they see it as we do, from the comfort of our high-tech homes, or should we expect radically different insights from our own? How will we relearn our readings of Scripture in the light of the experience of so many in the body of Christ in the two thirds world today? Should we look west, or east and south?

Exporting church

Those of us who have originated in historically imperialist and exporting countries such as the UK and USA have got used to the idea that apparently strong 'Christian' nations will include in their populations church leaders who believe that God has called them to publish abroad their paradigms of Christian mission, spirituality, worship, and service to other nations which they believe have not benefited from the light of the gospel as long as they have, or to those where they think that the church is in decline. Today, the traffic is from west to east, mostly from North

America to Europe and the Middle and Far East, and south to the growing churches of sub-Saharan Africa, South Asia and South America ('the South'). Mass printed publications, the expansion of internet access, and improvement of telephone lines and other forms of telecommunication have facilitated this flow. Yet the churches of the West are very poor at welcoming a reversal of such currents. We find it hard to receive inspiration from the church in Cambodia, or Cote d'Ivoire, or Colombia. We tend to think that we are the strong and they are the weak, and that we must make allowances for their relative immaturity in faith and Christian living. The headquarters of many major Christian agencies are still firmly in Western countries. We do not expect the church in the non-Western world to be making significant impacts on the enculturated evils which we perceive to be at the heart of many of their nations, such as political corruption, bribery, and the abuse of women and children. Western leaders have really been inviting others to look west, rather than themselves looking east and south. In fact, they have been militantly trying to export Western democratic systems through regime change.

It seems to me that this flies in the face of Peter's worldview and world vision, as expressed in 1 Peter. He did not set himself up as all wise and all knowing, with nothing to learn from the churches to which he was writing in Asia Minor. Rather, he saw the process of communication as two-way. He was hoping to receive as much as he was able to give, recognizing that he had much to learn from what God was doing at the frontiers of Christian mission, on the eastern fringes of the Roman Empire. Certainly, as he was writing from Rome, on the verge of the Neronian persecution, and would soon be martyred for Christ, his theme of coping with trials was not mere theoretical reflection. Nevertheless, he holds up the Christians of Asia Minor as examples for his apostolic team and the Roman church to follow. 'These [trials] have come so that your faith . . . may be proved genuine and may result in praise, glory, and honour when Jesus Christ is revealed. Though you have not seen him, you love him; and even though you do not see him now, you believe in him and are filled with an inexpressible and glorious joy' (1:7–8). Peter had had the inestimable privilege of living and working with

Jesus of Nazareth, and of being an eyewitness of his risen life. But their faith 'of greater worth than gold' (v. 7) was shining in a dark situation and setting an example for Christians everywhere, despite the fact that they had never met Christ in person, nor had they seen or touched his resurrected body. Peter's ethical exhortations are rooted in the conviction that God is at work among the believers to whom he writes, and that they need to let God deepen and develop their faith and witness, individually and corporately. He wrote to the elders of the churches, challenging them to be what they were already, only more so, as a fellow elder (5:1), shepherd, and superintendent (5:2). He wrote with the help of Silas (5:12) and Mark (5:13), summarizing his message as 'encouraging you and testifying that this is the true grace of God. Stand fast in it' (5:12). Their experience of suffering for the gospel was exemplary, and an inspiration to the whole church, and not merely to their local little flocks. God's grace is not cheap, as Dietrich Bonhoeffer reminded us before his suffering at the hands of the Nazis. God's grace is free, yet, paradoxically, priceless and costly.[7] 'And the God of all grace, who called you to his eternal glory in Christ, after you have suffered a little while, will himself restore you and make you strong, firm and steadfast' (5:10).

The good news of God's gracious work was at the heart of Peter's preaching and paraenesis, as we have seen, and his leading of the church was always in response to that. His paradigm of Christian leadership related to 'God's elect . . . chosen according to the foreknowledge of God' (1:1–2), with the hope 'Grace and peace be yours in abundance' (1:2). That meant simply that, at that particular moment in history, God was graciously at work in a special way in the regions within which they lived. It was important for them to ride the wave of God's mission among them, and to ensure that the work which had begun would continue, despite the pressures they were under to conform to the values of the non-Christian populace among whom they lived. The hope is that their obedience, and especially that of their leaders, would ensure that the gospel had a long-term future in Pontus, Galatia, Cappadocia, Asia and Bithynia. We know that the churches of Asia Minor flourished for six centuries after the time of Peter, until the rise and spread of Islam in the seventh century CE. Today there are very few indigenous Christians in the

country now known as Turkey. Eventually, it seems that heresy
and false teaching weakened the witness of these churches and
made them susceptible to the influx of Islam and a message
which does not focus on grace but on law. As the church struggled with divisions and the move of the imperial centre of government from Rome to Byzantium (Constantinople, today
Istanbul), the two-way communications established in Peter's
time clearly became a thing of the past. Instead, the rise of domineering episcopacy, and eventually of the Roman papacy,
replaced the dynamic forms of Christian leadership which Peter
and his associates had established. So, in a strange way, the
churches of Asia Minor became examples of what not to do, just
as Peter himself had known personally, to his cost. The churches
were vulnerable fellowships of forgiven sinners like himself, constantly in need of God's gracious forgiveness and renewal, to
deal with bouts of doubting, denial and desertion, in the same
way that he himself had been in need.

And so the dialogue continues. We look east to what we imagine is the absence of the true God, and ask questions of believers
long dead so that we might learn from their mistakes as well as
from their achievements for Christ and his Kingdom.

The church as paradigm – the Way

The concept of paradigm also fits in with the early Christian title
for the church – 'The Way' – which was particularly associated
with Paul's mission and ministry, and appears a number of times
in Acts 9 – 24. The idea is that believers demonstrate the gospel
in the way they live their lives, following Jesus who called himself 'The Way, the Truth, and the Life' (Jn. 14:6). In addition, Peter
refers to Christianity as 'the way of truth' in 2 Peter 2:2, and contrasts the model of true Christian behaviour and belief with that
of false prophets and false teachers who have infiltrated the
church and will continue to do so. 'Many will follow their
depraved conduct and will bring the way of truth into disrepute.
In their greed these teachers will exploit you with fabricated stories . . . These people are springs without water and mists driven
by a storm . . . For they mouth empty, boastful words, and by

appealing to the lustful desires of sinful human nature, they entice people who are just escaping from those who live in error' (2 Pet. 2:2, 17–18). Peter's way, therefore, is the proper paradigm, true to the teaching and practice of Christ and the apostolic teams, and dependent on spiritual revelation and illumination, unlike the stories which imposters have concocted and imposed upon weak believers. Christianity is a way of life which claims to be the true way; the way that really expresses God's will for humankind, setting examples for unbelievers to follow and become part of the paradigm. Christian leaders are called to motivate their communities not by their own intentions, imaginations, and desires, but by the truth, theological and ethical, into which the risen Lord is leading his church by his Spirit.

Today, Peter's way primarily involves a radical determination to teach and live by the above-mentioned revealed truths, the word of God which is contained in the Scriptures of Old and New Testaments. In fact, Peter's focus here is rooted in Psalm 119:29–32: 'Keep me from deceitful ways; be gracious to me and teach me your law. I have chosen the way of faithfulness (truth); I have set my heart on your laws. I hold fast to your statutes, LORD; do not let me be put to shame. I run in the path of your commands, for you have set my heart free.'

So Peter's paradigm fits in with the emphases of other apostles like Paul, while always providing examples of holistic Christian living, in word and deed. Peter's way for the church today is focused on paraenesis (ethical exhortation); the call of God to godly lifestyles, each step along the path of life, individually and corporately, as exemplified in his life and those of his colleagues, but especially in the churches which he had planted or developed in Asia Minor. The motivation for that is not a raft of worldly-wise, empty promises which might appeal to the darker side of our human nature. New converts were, and are, susceptible to the appeals which such infiltrators make to the churches in order to draw them back into error and sin. Christian leaders, for example, have often made the mistake of trying to motivate their people by guilt manipulation. They have preached sermons which play on people's sense of inadequacy and failure. They have adopted counselling strategies which focus on confronting specific sins as the cause of every emotional or motivational problem. They have taught believers to parent their children in a similar way, with the result that many Christians, Catholic as well as evangelical, have grown up struggling with guilt feelings which can paralyse their lives with fear, remorse and dread, even though they have confessed their sin and placed their trust in Christ as Saviour and Lord.

Let me expand on this for a moment. Professor of Psychology Bruce Narramore has exposed the above strategy in a seminal book[8] which should be recommended reading for every pastor, as well as for all concerned Christian parents. He distinguishes between guilt feelings and constructive sorrow, following Paul's teaching in 2 Corinthians 7:10: 'Godly sorrow brings repentance that leads to salvation and leaves no regret, but worldly sorrow brings death.' He shows that it is possible to learn to motivate oneself and others without playing on guilt feelings, while affirming true penitence as a healthy and ongoing process which is part of psychological and spiritual renewal. Concerning motivation in preaching Narramore writes:

> I would suggest several guidelines that can help pastors and others who teach and speak to avoid creating unnecessary guilt in our hearers. 1. Set realistic standards for parishioners. 2. Minister to meet the needs of the congregation. 3. Stress our position in Christ and what he has done for us. 4. Involve people in planning programmes and projects. 5. Balance conviction with encouragement and forgiveness. 6. Distinguish between God's firm but loving correction of his children and the wrathful punishment those who reject Christ are under. 7. Do not scold or preach in anger, but 'Speak the truth in love' (Ephesians 5:15). 8. Evaluate our own attitudes as speakers to see that we are not attempting to manipulate our hearers. 9. Try to offer concrete steps to regular growth instead of vague formulas and challenges. 10. Model a humble acknowledgment of our own failures.[9]

That is what Peter modelled in his first letter. His ethical challenge is not mere moralism – 'It's nice to be nice, and good to be good.' It is rooted in the Christian hope which flows from the resurrection of Jesus Christ from the dead. In fact, hope is the supreme motivation which Peter uses throughout this piece of writing:

Praise be to the God and Father of our Lord Jesus Christ! In his great mercy he has given us new birth into a living hope through the resurrection of Christ from the dead (1:3) . . . Set your hope on the grace to be brought to you when Jesus Christ is revealed at his coming (1:13) . . . Through him you believe in God, who raised him from the dead and glorified him, and so your faith and hope are in God (1:21) . . . For this is the way the holy women of the past who put their hope in God used to adorn themselves (3:5) . . . Always be prepared to give an answer to everyone who asks you to give the reason for the hope that you have' (3:15).

Leadership and Christian hope

It is here that we do well to look east. Raymond Fung, from Hong Kong, worked for the World Council of Churches Commission on World Mission and Evangelism, and wrote a brief but strategic book based on Isaiah's vision as recorded in Isaiah 65:17–25, a text which includes this prophecy: 'The LORD says, "I am making a new earth and new heavens . . . The new Jerusalem I make will be full of joy . . . Babies will no longer die in infancy . . . Like trees, my people will live long lives. They will fully enjoy the things they have worked for . . . I will answer their prayers"' (NIV). This is full of hope for the future, yet is still elusive for many millions in the world today. Churches have worked together to serve and advocate the cause of the powerless for many years, but often without moving on to the invitation to worship and discipleship, Fung notes. 1 Peter 3:15 shows this, he says:

> That we are to give an account of our hope to others presupposes that Christians are accountable to the world . . . Why? . . . Being accountable means being answerable to the world for our belief and our actions. We have the obligation to explain to people what we believe and what we do not believe, why we act in a certain way and not in other ways. Christians are not obliged to do what others tell us but we are under obligation to explain our convictions and actions. By so doing we affirm our Christian identity and at the same time strengthen our ties with others outside the church . . . Peter suggests to us that the account Christians are to give is

the account of our hope. It is not to be an account of our past and present achievement, personal or corporate. It is to be an account of what we dearly wish to be and become. The cutting edge of Christian testimony is not the perfection of our moral conduct, nor the success of our individual and corporate living. In our testimony, according to Peter, what will be inviting to others is our hope – that which is yet to be, that which we long to see happen, that which we strive to become.[10]

This is in sharp contrast to the 'look west' philosophy exemplified by such movements as Rick Warren's 'Purpose Driven' approach, where evidence of success, as seen in dramatic numerical growth and various tangible outcomes, is supreme. The fact that this approach has become a brand which is protected by registered trade marks should be a real concern for Christian leaders, notwithstanding the fact that Warren's books contain much useful and relevant material. The idea that the Christian life and the church can be branded in this way reveals much about the orientation of such key motivators, and their need, with the rest of us, radically to learn from Peter's paradigm.

Philip Yancey reflects on the different attitudes to prayer that he witnessed in conversation with Americans and Japanese:

> A Japanese Christian told me that on her first trip to the US she was shocked by the directness of our prayers. The American pray-er, she said, resembles a person who goes to Burger King and orders a 'Whopper, well done, but hold the pickle and lettuce, with extra ketchup, please.' The Japanese is more like the tourist who walks into a foreign restaurant unable to read the menu. He finally communicates, with gestures and a reference to a phrase book, that he would like the house speciality . . . You never know what you will get, for the host determines it.[11]

In contrast with this Japanese attitude, many people buy the 'Purpose Driven' brand books and ancillary materials because they want to experience the kind of results which have already been manifested. They want to be assured that their prayers will be answered in accordance with the brand formula. They want to benefit from the market share of the brand! Peter's way is quite different, and is encouraging to those of us who are aware of our failures yet earnestly desire to see others receive Christ and become part of his church. Fung reminds us that evangelism requires us to present our Christian hope and our determination to press on towards its fulfilment:

> Our struggle towards God and towards what God wants to see happen in this world invites others to identification with us . . . I think Christians giving an account of our hope includes giving an account of our limitations, weaknesses, fears and even failures . . . We come before the world as we are, human, broken and fearful, like everyone else, but always pressing on and always living in hope.[12]

Fung goes on to tell the story of a female lay evangelist in South India who had been working in a poor parish for many years, serving, preaching, and refusing offers of greener pastures, yet with few indications that any of her parishioners were keen to follow in the Christian way. Then, at a meeting with a group of girls who had left home because they feared being sold into prostitution, she burst out in anger: 'The one thing that will liberate you . . . is the gospel . . . yet to it you have shown no response.' Then one of the girls timidly put up her hand and said: 'You have been so patient and so good to us we thought we could never be like you. We can never be good enough to be Christian.' Fung says that proved to be a new beginning in that evangelist's mission and ministry among the poor. He cites another situation, in New Zealand, of a downtown congregation committed to serving the urban poor indigenous (Maori) people. A group of unemployed young people in the district asked for financial help and a place to meet, and the congregation was divided over what to do in response. 'At some point it became clear that even if the congregation were able to come to one mind, it would not have the resources to meet the increasing demands made on its limited resources. The answer was found in Peter's statement about giving account of our hope. The congregational leadership, divided on this particular issue, decided to try out Peter's advice.'[13] What happened next was an example of 'look east' thinking. They admitted to the young people that they couldn't agree on what to do in response to their request. So they asked them to attend the next congregational meeting and share in the debate if they wanted to. The leaders confessed that the division was not a good reflection on the church, but that they needed to give account of themselves to the young people. Never before had church members discussed any issue in the presence of non-members, and particularly something which had a direct bearing on the latter. The meeting was packed and lasted three hours, with frankness and honesty on both sides. Some Christians complained about the 'blunt language and arrogant behaviour'[14] of the youth group. The needs of disadvantaged young people were presented by those with first-hand experience. 'The liberality of God and the limitations of Christians were expressed in painful reflections. The congregation, warts and all, was giving an account of its hope and . . . of its struggles and weaknesses.'[15] Through this process a solution emerged. A small amount of money was set aside, and conditions were agreed, on the basis of mutual accountability. The group set up its office in a small room in the church buildings. Two years later it became the official youth fellowship of the church and continued to engage in a dynamic outreach to the young people of the area. Fung concludes, 'Giving an account of our hope is both an expression of our solidarity with our neighbours, and an invitation to them to examine for themselves the Christian faith.'[16]

Preach the gospel, not your church

Enabling others to examine the faith means living, preaching and teaching the good news of God's kingdom, together as God's people. As Lesslie Newbigin said, 'The congregation is the hermeneutic of the gospel',[17] which means that unbelievers learn from the way churches exist and act out the essence of the Christian message, rather than through some individualistic appropriation of abstract theology. That may seem a truism, but it needs to be said.

But that does not mean that the gospel is defined by the stories of individual congregations, church groupings, or denominations. Let me explain. Twenty years ago, when I was serving in a large housing scheme parish in the city of Perth, Scotland, the local presbytery received a letter from Mike MacDonald, a pastor of a growing church in California, which met in a cinema, following the formula of many expanding evangelical churches at that time. Mike said that he was of Scottish origin, and felt that God wanted him to come to Scotland to encourage the churches here. He was so convinced of the rightness of his offer that he came over with a colleague to share his vision with a group of church leaders. I remember that meeting vividly. We were impressed by Mike's humility and desire to serve as he told us of what was happening back home in California. I was about ten years into my ministry at the time, and chairing the presbytery local mission committee. After we had heard Mike's presentation, which I found to be very challenging and exciting, I immediately shared my response that we should invite Mike and his team to come over and tell us what God was doing in his church. However, an older colleague and good friend, Sandy, who had been in the presbytery for over twenty years, begged to differ. 'No,' he said, 'Let's invite Mike to come over and preach the gospel!' Of course, there is a difference between the gospel and the apparent success story of any contemporary, or historic, church.

Even in the New Testament, the gospel is not presented as a message which focuses on model congregations and ideal methods of church growth. In 1 Peter there is no attempt to single out the church in Rome as an example for the churches in Asia Minor to follow. That is quite significant, given that Paul had written his long letter to the Romans probably some seven years earlier and had visited Rome in defence of his mission, when he presented his case before Caesar. He had, after two years or so under house arrest, been acquitted and released for a fourth missionary journey, and had travelled to new places like Crete, where he left Titus in charge, and revisited churches which he had established in Greece and Asia Minor. Peter had arrived in Rome again after that time, we believe, and was surely aware of the strategic importance of Christians living in the capital city of a vast empire. Yet the first letter of Peter does not mention the Roman Christians until the very end, where there is only a brief coded greeting: 'She who is in Babylon, chosen together with you, sends you her greetings' (5:13). In this way, Peter connected the work of God in Rome with the mission at the outposts of the eastern Empire, expressing solidarity with believers everywhere. They were resident aliens and marginalized by a state and societies, on the verge of a severe persecution of Christians. Rome was 'Babylon' as much as the Mesopotamian city of that name had been, which had waged war on Jerusalem and enslaved/exiled its people. But the growing church in Rome was not to be followed. Jesus Christ is the only valid and universal model of true humanity, holy lifestyle, individual and corporate faith, church leadership, and community creation and care, as exemplified in his three-year ministry and through the lives and witnessing of the apostles, in whom he continued his work by the power of the Holy Spirit. Jesus is the good news personified. We don't need to preach our church; we need to preach the Christ.[18]

The propaganda of success

That affirmation is easily lost in the current climate, where certain church leaders are setting up themselves and their ministries, along with the stories of what they believe God is doing in and through their churches, as detailed examples which they believe any church anywhere can and should follow. That is not the gospel. There is no secret formula which needs to be exported, with seven habits or forty days of action or any other secret strategy as the ultimate solution to church leadership and numerical growth. In fact, what is claimed as success may well turn out to be failure in the long term, and vice versa. Consider these notable examples:

- Paderewski, the great Polish pianist, was once told by his music teacher that his hands were much too small to master the keyboard.
- The great Italian tenor Enrico Caruso was told by his teacher, early in the twentieth century, that his voice 'sounded like the wind whistling through the window'.
- When the Victorian British MP and future Prime Minister, Benjamin Disraeli, attempted to speak in Parliament for the

first time, members hissed him into silence and laughed when he said, 'Though I sit down now, the time will come when you will hear me.'

- During his career in Africa, David Livingstone, nineteenth-century Scottish missionary and explorer, made only one convert, who subsequently lapsed from Christian commitment.[19]
- Henry Ford forgot to put a reverse gear in his first car.
- In 1905 the University of Bern, Switzerland, turned down a PhD. dissertation as being irrelevant and fanciful. Its author was one Albert Einstein.[20]
- In 2005 the doctor who invented the Atkins Diet died, weighing 18 stone! He had found a very large market in the Western world for the belief that one could eat large amounts of protein, and few carbohydrates, fruit or vegetables, and yet lose significant amounts of weight, thus standing on its head the conventional wisdom of a balanced diet. But his own demise was self-contradictory!

As I have noted already, as I look back over thirty years of ministry, there have been wave upon wave of movements emanating from North America which have been acclaimed as God's prophetic sign to the rest of us. Today, virtually all of them have been subsumed into new denominations which contain almost as many traditions as the mainstream denominations, often suffering from power struggles and splits. Twenty years ago many of their leaders announced the demise of the traditional churches, and that the future was theirs alone. Today, few are quite so self-assured. One notable leader of the house church movement in Birmingham, England, has recently also become a canon of an Anglican cathedral! And yet new waves continue to arise and lap our shores, announcing the arrival of the way to be church in the twenty-first century, like a seasonal tsunami.

Friends, the Way is an open secret. It does not depend on our being recipients of the latest trends from the west. Peter's way of being and doing church is not the emerging church of dreams,[21] but the radical, long-term announcement and application of the word of God as revealed through the apostles and prophets. Every earnest pastor-teacher has access to the truths which can set God's people free, and church leaders are called together to establish congregations which reflect the love of God in Christ, the manifestation of his grace and power, rather than to mimic strategies which may have proved effective in totally different social and cultural settings. To follow Peter, as he followed his Lord, is not to lord it but to try to be a good example for God's people and those around us.

Leading examples look east and embrace Peter's paradigm. That, of course, does not mean literally looking to the geographical east, or south, or wherever, as the potential source of inspiration for our common mission. It means looking away from the global centres of apparent success and power, to the fringes, the marginalized, the poor, the oppressed. It is there that God is speaking most loudly, as C.S. Lewis once observed (that God whispers in our times of peace and shouts in our times of pain). Far from exporting what we imagine are self-evidently good models of church or spirituality from a position of perceived strength, we need to dialogue with, and listen to, the struggling saints in nations like China. David Aikman has written a book which should also be on every church leader's bookshelf, and in its final chapter he says this, with which we draw this chapter to a close:

> Worth noting is how the emergence of China as a Christianized nation will affect global Christendom itself. Some have argued that, if China's Protestant Christian population is close to 70 million, it would make China's Protestants one of the largest such communities in the world. There is bound to be a consequence from the powerful position globally that China has come to occupy. A thoughtful biographer of Wang Mingdao puts it this way: 'Regardless of which policy the Chinese government pursues, the church in China will profoundly affect the shape of Christianity worldwide for generations to come. With some thirty to seventy million souls and a growth rate of 7 percent annually, the number of Christians in China dwarfs the number of Christians in most nations of the earth. Like Christians throughout the developing world, Chinese Christians represent the vanguard of the church in the 21st century.[22]

It is with that vision, which I hope is resonant with the remainder of this book, that I challenge church leaders, existing and potential, to learn to lead by example – Peter's way.

Summary

In this final chapter we have focused on seven key themes which the whole book explores in detail:

- The concept of paradigm shift in Christian mission as promoted by Bosch shows that we can choose from various paradigms and engage with historic Christian tradition in the expectation also of being surprised.
- We need to learn readings of 1 Peter which resonate with the experience of poor and exploited believers in the South today (i.e. Africa south of the Sahara, South and East Asia, South America).
- Western Christians must be very wary of trying to export their forms of church uncritically to the South without seeking first to learn from their churches, many of which have a long history.
- Peter's paradigm emphasizes that Christianity involves a way of life rather than merely a series of dogmas.
- It is a hopeful way of life motivated by the grace of the gospel and informed by godly sorrow for sin rather than by the intentional cultivation of guilt feelings.
- Christian leaders everywhere need to learn to motivate believers by modelling and teaching real Christian hope, examples of which are particularly found among Christians of the South.
- *SelfEvidentSuccessSystems* adopted by churches and church leaders are characterized by self-referential propagandas of success and must be questioned and qualified by longer-term reflection on the real outcomes experienced, rather than soon after an initial period of apparent effectiveness.

Conclusion

Next Steps for Leaders and Learners

Next steps for leaders – ongoing restoration and renewal (Jn. 21:1–19)

The different denominations have various titles for church leaders, as we have noted. In our Presbyterian and Reformed tradition it is ministers (or pastors) and elders (plus deacons in some situations). In Episcopalian, Orthodox and Catholic churches it is bishops, priests and deacons. In Baptist churches it is pastors and deacons, and some have elders, too. Some independent churches just have elders. In this book we have focused on the full-time or part-time ministry and mission of priests, pastors and ministers as well as of those called elders who exercise a teaching ministry. This reflects the guidelines laid down in the New Testament for establishing leadership teams led by those who are 'able to teach' (1 Tim. 3:2; 2 Tim. 2:24, cf. 1 Pet. 4:11a; 5:1–4). It must wait for another discussion to explore the nature and purpose of the other forms of church leadership found in the New Testament and in the churches today. As we have seen, Peter's understanding of pastoral leadership is that it is a team effort encouraged and developed by committed team leaders.

But all Christian team leadership must ultimately be traced back to the story found in John 21, the moving account of the restoration of Simon Peter to a foundational leading role in the early church, despite his threefold denial of Jesus before the crucifixion. It followed the amazing repeat of a feat which Christ had accomplished at the beginning of his mission (Lk. 5:1ff) when he had called four fishermen to follow him: his ability to know where shoals of fish could be found, despite the fact that he was a joiner and builder by trade! This time Peter dragged the net ashore and they counted 153 fish! Jesus made breakfast for them on the beach and proved beyond any reasonable doubt, for the third time since the first Easter, that he had really risen from death. Peter's encounter with Jesus teaches us much of importance about Christian team leading. We leaders need a fresh encounter with Christ.

Delegating

The first thing we have to recognize about Christian team leadership is that it is delegated by the risen Christ to those whom he calls to take on the responsibility of overseeing the life and work of Christian churches. Those of us who have accepted ordination as minister, pastor, priest or elder must realize that we have no authority to lead in ourselves. We have not been chosen because we are worthy or are individually up to the task. We are called to share in Christ's mission and ministry to the world through his church. For forty days he appeared to the first disciples to prove that he really is alive for evermore. Then he empowered his people, as he had promised he would, when the gift of the Holy Spirit was outpoured at Pentecost, fifty days after the resurrection. Christian leaders – called in the New Testament apostles, prophets, evangelists, elders/overseers and deacons – were charged to carry on the work that Jesus had begun. They were to pass on the message about the kingdom of God and, in fellowship with other believers, to build communities of faith which are founded on truth and love by the grace of God. Because people were faithful to that task down through the generations we are Christians today, worshipping God in spirit and in truth. That is the true apostolic succession – not the passing on of some mysterious influence by the laying on of the hands of a bishop, but the faithful transmission and re-enactment of the word of God which is fulfilled in the life, death and resurrection of Jesus, wherever it is proclaimed in the power of the Spirit for the glory of the Father. In other words, when God's people are willing to be led by the Lord, he will raise up Christian leaders and delegate to them the ongoing tasks of spearheading evangelism, Bible teaching, pastoral care and ethical exhortation. That's why, from the beginning, Peter and the others were challenged by Jesus, 'Follow me!'

That means, 'Do what I do. Say what I say. Care as I care. Live as I live.'

So this is the first hallmark of Christian leadership in the community of the resurrection which is the church. We ministers accept Christ's delegation of the tasks which he wants to continue to do through us, and we in turn delegate and share those tasks among the people of God. We say to all, in Christ's name, 'Follow him!', and are called to set an example. In fact, leading by example is the truly Christian approach. That does not mean that elders, ministers, pastors or priests are called to do all the tasks and that the other members are just spectators of their work. Ministers are not middlemen who alone can mediate God's mission and ministry. As we have seen, Peter was later to teach the 'priesthood of all believers' in his first letter to Christians in a number of churches throughout what is now called Turkey: 'You are a chosen people, a royal priesthood, a holy nation, a people belonging to God, that you may declare the praises of him who called you out of darkness into his wonderful light' (1 Pet. 2:9).

Loving

The second thing we notice about Christian team leadership from John 21 is that it is about loving. Peter was asked first of all whom he loved the most. Did he love Jesus more than he loved his fellow fishermen? Or did he love Jesus more than they did? Was he prepared to put that love on the line and prove it in sacrificial service, if necessary giving up his day job to go full-time as a missionary? The same question is put to potential and existing leaders today. Jesus asks us, 'Do you truly love me more?' (21:16, NIV). This refers to a love in which one's entire personality and will are involved, including a spontaneous supernatural affection or fondness which transcends mere liking or admiring. Such is the importance of loving Jesus that he asks the question three times: 'Do you truly love me . . . do you . . . do you?' Of course, that threefold repetition had special significance for Peter, as he had denied that he knew Jesus on three occasions before dawn on the first Good Friday. But we are to see ourselves as in the shoes of Simon Peter. Like him, we are tempted to back off and run away from the call of God when things get tough. Like him, we so easily break our promises of faithfulness to God. It is so much easier to talk and write about Christian faith and about taking a lead than to live it out. So we need to be reminded every day of Christ's call to put him first in our lives in terms of commitment of our time, talents and money, especially if we have accepted ordination or its equivalent. Like Peter, we will be hurt because Jesus continues to ask the same question of us. True love does hurt. Christian leadership is costly: 9 April is the anniversary of the execution of Dietrich Bonhoeffer, less than a month before the end of World War II, for the part that he played in the German resistance as a minister in the Confessing Church. His book *The Cost of Discipleship* had been published in 1938, and he had had the chance to live and work in America and be out of danger. But he believed that God was calling him to return to Germany and continue the moral, spiritual and political struggle against the evil of Nazism. He was arrested in 1943 and his letters and papers from prison over the next two years before his death were to become a powerful testimony for Christian people everywhere, and a collection of them is still in print today. As Peter said, Jesus knows all things and he knows whether we really love him. In his first letter he says, 'Above all, love one another deeply, because love covers over a multitude of sins . . . If you speak you should do so as one speaking the very words of God. If you serve, you should do so with the strength God provides' (1 Pet. 4:8–11). That refers to the two main aspects of leading: speaking and serving. Christ's love covered Peter's many sins, and he does the same for us. Christian leaders are far from perfect and make many mistakes, but love conquers all.

Teaching

Then the third thing which John 21 teaches about Christian team leadership is equally important. Leaders have been delegated their tasks by Jesus and must learn to delegate. They are followers and call others to follow Jesus. Leaders really love Jesus and his people and call others to do the same. But how do they set about achieving that? By taking good care of the flock. This is how they will grow in their faith and practical commitment. In his first letter, Peter uses a similar analogy: 'Like newborn babies, crave the pure milk of the word, so that by it you may grow up in your salvation, now that you have tasted that the Lord is good'

(1 Pet. 2:2–3, my translation). Therefore, properly feeding God's hungry children is the supreme way to take care of God's people, the church, through good teaching: 'Feed my lambs . . . Feed my sheep.' That's why Paul was so keen for Timothy to find people who were 'able to teach'. We see from this that it is impossible to be a good minister without emphasizing and faithfully exercising the ministry of the word. There are many demands on our time, but this – what the apostles called prayer and the ministry of the word (Acts 6:4) – must always have the top priority. When they were struggling with meeting the needs of a large and growing congregation in Jerusalem, they delegated the practical care of widows to others (Acts 6:1–6). The result was, as Luke says, that 'The word of God continued to spread; the number of the disciples increased greatly in Jerusalem, and a great many of the priests became obedient to the faith' (6:7, NRSV). Luke saw the connection between the apostles' delegation and effective outreach among Jewish priests, who were clearly impressed by the sharing of responsibilities. To some in the church today, the hallmark of the effective minister is rushing around doing as many of the tasks of the church himself or herself, including social visiting, so that others may applaud (or boo) from the sidelines. If that means that the minister has too little time to prepare for worship and preaching, that does not seem to matter. In contrast, preacher and people are together called to practise what is preached and actively to embody the message which is incarnate in Christ crucified and risen.

But the first priority is the in-depth ministry of the word. No mother considers herself to be doing a good job if her children are poorly fed, even if she is frantically rushing around trying to promote many other things which are good for children, like education, sporting activities, and wholesome entertainment. She and her husband will spend a lot of time planning and preparing nourishing meals to ensure a balanced diet for a growing healthy child. The result of failing to do that is seen today in the epidemic of childhood obesity, often the result of too much convenience food and too many ready-cooked meals. The same is true of the church, God's children. We all need the spiritual feeding which comes through the careful preparation and serving of the word of God, week by week. We all need to experience for ourselves the meeting of our deepest needs and the developing of an appetite for the truth and wisdom of God's word, along with practical guidance and direction as to how best to put into practice what we are learning. We are sheep and lambs that need feeding. Jesus is the Good Shepherd, and we who are leaders are called to share in his shepherding, especially through teaching and preaching.

Moving forward as leaders

Delegating . . . loving . . . teaching . . . the core attitudes and activities of the effective Christian team leader in which every growing believer will want to be involved, to the glory of God and for the good of his people. Peter learned that from the risen Lord Jesus when he was restored to his leadership position as an apostle. Jesus modelled that, and Peter learned, the hard way, to lead by example. Peter's restoration enabled him to recover from tendencies to domineer over his fellow disciples, as on those occasions recorded in the Gospel of Mark where he impetuously blurted out pledges of commitment ('Even if all fall away, I will not', Mk. 14:29); claimed the role of sole spokesman for the disciples, despite his frequent gaffs ('"Rabbi, it is good for us to be here. Let us put up three shelters – one for you, one for Moses and one for Elijah." He did not know what to say', Mk. 9:5); and even set about trying to dissuade Jesus from completing his mission on the cross ('Peter took him aside and began to rebuke him. But when Jesus turned and looked at his disciples, he rebuked Peter. "Get behind me Satan, You do not have in mind the concerns of God, but merely human concerns"', Mk. 8:32–33).

If we are Christian leaders, or aspire to leadership, we must continually seek restoration and renewal as we determine to put into practice the principles learned through our study of 1 Peter and its implications for twenty-first-century churches. If we are being led, then we must encourage that process, and recognize the rightful authority of those women and men whom God has called to oversee his work in the world. Leading by example, modelled by suffering shepherds (2 Pet. 1:14; 1 Pet. 5:2–3), is an urgent priority for every congregation of God's people, the disciples (learners) of Jesus. All are learners, but some are called to lead by example.

Next steps for learners – living the Christian life (1 Pet. 3:8–18)

In this book, with Peter's guidance, we have focused on what the church is, as the people of God with the purpose of proclaiming God's praise for all his mercy to us, in a world in which many are estranged from their Maker. We are all invited to gather week by week in God's presence, as congregations of the faithful, on Sunday, the Lord's Day. We Presbyterians sing praise, offer prayers, and then listen to the message from God's word, before praying for others, praising God's name and pronouncing God's blessing. That is the familiar pattern of public worship in our Reformed tradition, and is reflected in other denominations and fellowships. It is rooted in the rhythms of which we have read in the New Testament, not least from letters like 1 Peter, which were written in order to be read aloud in the churches, then to be explained and applied to the current situations of those involved in Christian witness and service. 1 Peter is really all about living the Christian life, as our response to what God has done for us in Christ. Peter urges us strongly 'to abstain from sinful desires' and to 'live such good lives among the pagans . . . that they may see your good deeds and glorify God' (2:11,12).

But what is 'the good life'? How would you answer that question? Some say that the good life is a life which causes no harm to others, but that sounds a bit negative and passive. Others suggest that the good life contributes to the well-being of humanity and leaves this world in a better state than one finds it. But that sounds very vague and hard to measure. So a third approach might be to look at our productivity – whether we live lives which enhance wealth or some other benefit, like education, or health. Yet some of the most famous lives which we would think of as good, might not be open to such assessment. A fourth answer might focus on virtue, and assess the good life as displaying certain qualities, such as courage, loyalty, kindness, or love. We could go on, because everybody has her or his ideas about the good life, which may be dreams of living in different circumstances, fulfilling aspirations which are as yet beyond our reach. That's why home relocation programmes are so popular on television today.

Thankfully, Peter does not leave us in the lurch! He knows what he means by the good life. It is the Christian life, the life of good deeds which glorify God as Jesus did. It is a life of following Christ, as Peter sought to do – imperfectly, but with the hope of getting better at it with time and effort. 'Live as servants of God' (2:16, NIV). It is a life lived in the real world, with its relationships, responsibilities, and rights; and if there is one word which encapsulates a Christian attitude to life, and informs all Christian action, it is respect. Peter shows us how proper respect must be shown to authorities, like kings or governments and their agents, even when they are despots as some emperors have been (3:13–17). Then he speaks about respect for employers, even when they are harsh in their dealings with employees (3:18–20). He goes on to speak of mutual respect between husbands and wives, especially when one partner is not as yet a believer. He stresses the equality of the partnership (3:1–7). Then he focuses on the church.

What does mutual respect look like in congregations of the faithful? How does it affect relationships, responsibilities, and rights? Again Peter urges all of us, without exception, to live in a certain way:

- Relationships characterized by living 'in harmony with one another (literally, of one mind, united in our attitude to life), sympathetic . . . (sharing feelings of joy and sorrow with one another), loving one another . . . (recognizing that we have one Father), compassionate . . . (with deep kindness for others in need)' (3:8). Here Peter (or his secretary, Silas) uses a string of Greek words which are found only here in the New Testament, which indicates how special are the relationships between real Christians in the church of Jesus Christ. He was literally lost for words! Are our relationships within our church so outstanding? Could it be said of us, as it was of the first Christians, 'See how they love one another'? How can we improve our caring and sharing? 'To this you were called so that you may inherit a blessing' (3:9). It is our Christian vocation and birthright to enjoy such a quality of life together, and we can't be satisfied until our relationships reflect that mutual respect.

- Responsibilities take shape as we learn to relate. The key is humility, which is about accepting a respectful and realistic view of one's significance and that of others in the fellowship. It is also the outstanding characteristic of the life of Jesus, who became humble for our sake. That means non-retaliation, and refusal to engage in trading insults or getting one's own back on others. In fact, abuse is an opportunity for peacemaking and seeking others' welfare (3:8–11). The church which enthusiastically accepts such responsibilities will attract others.
- Rights are expected in such a church, which are not claims for self but the gracious rewards of God freely bestowed on those who trust in him. The eyes of the Lord are upon them and he listens to their prayers, yet they may well suffer, at the hands of those who defy God's will, for doing right. Believers have no right to force their beliefs on others, but should be prepared to give reason for the hope that they share, with gentleness and respect (3:12–15). The church which shares these rights will grow, in quality and quantity.

But how is it possible to live such good lives? Why do some people respond wholeheartedly to Peter's exhortation to **live**! (3:8), to **love life**! (3:10) and to **do good**! (3:13) – while others seem to be lukewarm and relatively unmoved? The key is 3:15: 'In your hearts set apart Christ as Lord.' That means that our ultimate respect is for Jesus, so that our commitment is first and foremost to him. 'Set apart' here is from the same Greek verb as the one we use in the Lord's Prayer: 'Hallowed be thy name.' May there be a special relationship between each of us and our Lord Jesus, at the very core of our being – an inner commitment which will influence every decision we take and every action we make. Christian living is energized by the knowledge that Christ means more than anyone else or anything else in life for the believer. But why should that be? How can people be so committed to Christ?

'For Christ also suffered once for sins, the righteous for the unrighteous, to bring you to God. He was put to death in the body but made alive in the Spirit' (3:18). We can respect Christ above all, and respect others in his name, because of what happened on the cross and in the resurrection. Jesus was treated with the utmost disrespect. He took the blame for crimes he had never committed. He took the place of others who deserved punishment, and was despised and rejected, so that he cried in desolation, 'My God, why have you forsaken me?' (Mk. 15:34). He was separated from his Father, so that we might come to God and be able to experience acceptance, forgiveness, and fellowship. Peter felt that keenly, because he had denied three times that he even knew Christ, adding to his Master's sense of being abandoned. No amount of exhortation to do good is any good, in other words, unless it connects with Jesus' death and resurrection. We can live the Christian life only as we draw on the rhythms and resources which were made available then. Sin must be put to death in our mortal beings, and good living must be made alive by the power of his Spirit. We can live, love life, and do good. It's not a pipe-dream, if Jesus Christ is Lord of your life and mine, as we learn through those who are leading by example.

Take a look at the cover of this book as you put it down. The scene reminds me of Death Valley in California with the Sierra Nevada, or the high Sierra as it is sometimes called, in the background. The sand dunes there are always shifting with the winds. Footprints don't survive long, and those in this picture are coming towards the camera. As they get closer you can see that there is only one set of footprints. Past the point of contact, where the photographer stood, one can imagine joining the lone walker for the next stage of his journey. In the same way, Jesus is not calling us to follow him into the sunset by tracing his footsteps into the far distance but never hoping to catch up with him. Our journey of learning with Jesus begins with that personal encounter in penitence and faith when we meet with the Lord our Shepherd in the valley of deathly shadows (Ps. 23:4). The Lord will lead us out of dark experiences (and back into them, if he has a special purpose in it). The Lord who sent out his people into all the earth to make disciples (learners) also made a very wonderful promise to be with us until the end of time (Mt. 28:18–20). As we look back, the winds of time have blown away the footprints so that we can't dwell on what might have been. Peter has taught us that our journey with Jesus must always mean looking forward in faith. The best is yet to be. That's the hope of those who are really learning by example.

Endnotes

Introduction

1 Giuliani, *Leadership*.

1. Lording It

1 Pippert, *Hope has its reasons*, 5.
2 Christian Era.
3 See Marshall, *The Epistles of John*, 88–91.
4 Covey, *The 7 Habits of Highly Effective People*, 126.
5 Covey, *Living the 7 Habits*, frontispiece.
6 Covey, *Living*, frontispiece.
7 Covey, *Living*, frontispiece.
8 Lingenfelter and Mayers, *Ministering Cross-Culturally*.
9 *Catechism of the Catholic Church*, Second Edition English Translation.
10 Interestingly, the Latin *pontifex* literally means 'bridge-builder'.
11 *Catechism*, para. 880.
12 *Catechism*, para. 881.
13 *Catechism*, para. 882.
14 *Catechism*, paras. 886, 893.
15 Marshall, *1 Peter*, 21–4; Ellis, *The Making of the New Testament Documents*, 305ff. Cf. Kelly, *Commentary on the Epistles of Peter and Jude*, 26–34.
16 Thiede, *The Cosmopolitan World of Jesus*, 66–72, 100. See Jobes, *1 Peter*, 325–38.
17 Thiede, *Simon Peter*, 147.
18 Ellis, *Making*, 264ff, 366–76.

[19] Thiede, *Simon Peter*, 154ff. Paul speaks in Romans 16:7 of the prominent apostles Junia and Andronicus as being in Rome before Paul's first visit there. Bauckham, *Gospel Women*, 109ff identifies this couple as Joanna and Chuza of Luke's Gospel (Lk. 8:3, etc.).

[20] Thiede, *Simon Peter*, 167.

[21] Before the Christian Era.

[22] See Card, *A Fragile Stone*.

[23] See Thiede, *Simon Peter*, 17–25.

[24] See Hill, *Just Business*, 61–73.

[25] The former chairman of ICI put it in a nutshell when speaking of his own management style: 'I'm just a hired hack – a professional manager, I'm proud of that – I'm not a proprietor, not dominant. I lead by example and persuasion and a hell of a lot of hard work. Not on the basis of power or authority. My skills are to help a large number to release their energies and focus themselves. It is switching on a lot of people and helping them to achieve a common aim. People only do things they are convinced about. One has to create conditions in which people want to give of their best' (Haggai, *The Seven Secrets of Effective Business Relationships*, 96).

[26] 2 Corinthians 1:24: 'Not that we lord it over your faith, but we work with you for your joy.'

[27] Although later church leaders such as Augustine did, in a limited way – see ch. 4, endnote 13.

2. Strange Stories – Peter's and Ours

[1] 'Paraenesis . . . Exhortation. Passages with a strong exhortatory content in both OT and NT are termed paraenetic. The proclamation of Christ . . . and paraenesis are related to each other as gift and task, indicative and imperative, and in the realm of theological reflection as dogmatics and ethics' (Brown, ed. *New International Dictionary of NT Theology 1*, 65).

[2] See Kittel, ed., *Theological Dictionary of the New Testament*, VIII, 249f.

[3] 'One may conclude on good historical grounds that the extant literature of the Petrine mission consists of the Gospel of Mark composed in Caesarea c. 55–58 CE, 2 Peter in Caesarea 60–62 CE and 1 Peter in Rome 63–64 CE. 1 Peter represents both the final word of the great apostle and the closing chapter of his mission' (Ellis, *Making*, 306).

4 See Adair, *The Leadership of Jesus*; Griffiths, *The Example of Jesus*.

5 Thiede, *Simon Peter*, 52.

6 *Christos*, the Greek word for *Messiah*, was, of course, well established by the Septuagint, the Greek version of the Old Testament, which was well known in Galilee.

7 i.e. 'reckons'.

8 Stedman, *Body Life*.

9 See Walker, *Restoring the Kingdom*.

10 Wimber, *Power Evangelism*.

11 Watson, *I believe in the Church*.

12 See Robinson, *A World Apart*.

13 Warren, *The Purpose Driven Church*.

14 See Moynagh, *Changing World, Changing Church*; cf. Carson, *Becoming Conversant with the Emerging Church*.

15 The names used in these stories are not the individuals' real names.

16 Vitz, *Psychology as Religion*, 153.

17 Vitz, *Psychology*, 156.

18 Vitz, *Psychology*, 158.

19 'It is as if we automatically assume this is a naturally good world that has somehow been contaminated by evil. In terms of what we know of science, however, it is actually easier to explain evil. That things decay is quite explainable in accord with the natural law of physics. That life should evolve into more and more complex forms is not so easily understandable. That children generally lie and steal and cheat is routinely observable. The fact that sometimes they grow up to become truly honest adults is what seems more remarkable. Laziness is more the rule than diligence. If we seriously think about it, it probably makes more sense to assume this is a naturally evil world that has somehow been mysteriously "contaminated" by goodness, rather than the other way around. The mystery of goodness is even greater than the mystery of evil.' (Peck, *People of the Lie*, 41).

20 That does not rule out the Christian doctrine of *Christus Victor*, that believers may increasingly experience victory over sin, death, and the devil, through the work of Christ, as stated in the letters to the seven churches of Asia in Revelation 2 and 3: 'To those who are victorious I will give the right to eat from the tree of life, which is in the paradise of God . . . Those who are victorious will not be hurt at all by the second death . . . To those who are victorious, I will give some of the hidden manna . . . To all who are victorious, and do my will to

the end, I will give authority over the nations . . . Those who are victorious will, like them, be dressed in white. I will never blot out their names from the book of life . . . Those who are victorious I will make pillars in the temple of my God. Never again will they leave it . . . To those who are victorious, I will give the right to sit with me on my throne, just as I was victorious and sat with my Father on his throne' (Rev. 2:7, 11, 17, 26; 3:5, 12, 21).

3. Rhetoric and Resident Aliens

[1] Thurén, *Argument and Theology in 1 Peter*, 223.

[2] See the chapter 'The Congregation as Hermeneutic of the Gospel' in Newbigin, *The Gospel in a Pluralist Society*.

[3] See Houston, *Virtual Morality*, 81–91, 112–16.

[4] Thurén, *Argument*, 224.

[5] Thurén, *Argument*, 226.

[6] To say that someone is motivated is to say that he or she is willing to make the effort to reach a specific goal (Haggai, *Seven Secrets*, 94).

[7] Thurén, *Argument*, 227. See also Chester and Martin, T*he Theology of the Letters of James, Peter and Jude*, 87–133.

[8] Elliott, *A Home for the Homeless: a Sociological Exegesis of 1 Peter, its Situation and Strategy*. See also Meeks, *The First Urban Christians*; Harding, *Early Christian Life and Thought in Social Context*.

[9] The Greek translation of the Old Testament, allegedly the work of seventy Hebrew scholars in Alexandria, often abbreviated, or written alternatively, as LXX.

[10] Elliott, *Home*, 24.

[11] Elliott, *Home*, 25.

[12] Wright, *Deuteronomy*, 149. Also, 'God is love, so to walk in God's ways will entail the exercise of practical love, for ethics in the Old Testament, as much as in the New, involves the imitation of God' (p. 150).

[13] Wright, *Deuteronomy*, 151.

[14] Elliott, *Home*, 26.

[15] The Greek term used for the dispersion of Jews in other Mediterranean lands following various exiles from the Holy Land.

[16] Elliott, *Home*, 35.

[17] Elliott, *Home*, 38.

[18] Elliott, *Home*, 42.

[19] Elliott, *Home*, 45.

[20] Peter (1:1), Silas (5:12), and Mark (5:13).

[21] Elliott, *Home*, 47–8.

[22] Ephesians 3:14.

[23] Elliott, *Home*, 175

[24] Elliott, *Home*, 179

[25] Elliott, *Home*, 181

[26] Elliott, *Home*, 188

[27] These terms are clearly interchangeable in the New Testament. Paul greets the Philippian church, 'together with the overseers and deacons (Phil. 1:1), and issues instructions to Timothy in 1 Timothy 3:1–7 about the appointment of elders/overseers in the Ephesian church: 'Whoever aspires to be an overseer, desires a noble task.' Later he issues similar guidelines to Titus in Crete: 'Appoint elders in every town . . . since an overseer manages God's household . . .' (Tit. 1:5–9).

[28] See Ch. 5, endnote 2 for evidence that Priscilla was regarded by the early church as a presbyter.

[29] 'All you can do in motivating others is make as clear a link as possible between the goals you want them to share and the desires that most powerfully drive them. Get it wrong and you'll spark no interest at all. Get it right and they'll be motivating themselves' (Haggai, *Seven Secrets*, 96).

4. Elders and Shepherds

[1] Achtemeier, *1 Peter*, 24–5.

[2] Achtemeier, *1 Peter*, 26.

[3] Michaels, *1 Peter*, lxiv–lxv.

[4] Achtemeier, *1 Peter*, 27–8.

[5] Michaels, *1 Peter*, 276 (Michaels's translation).

[6] See Hurtado, *Mark*, 170–77.

[7] See Bennett, *Leadership Images from the New Testament*, 91–2; 173–6.

[8] 'Whoever speaks must do so as one speaking the very words of God; whoever serves must do so with the strength that God supplies' (NRSV).

[9] This assumes that 1 Timothy 5:17 does not distinguish between 'teaching' and 'ruling' elders, as historically some Presbyterians have

done, but that it refers to full-time elders (whose paid work is preaching) and part-time elders (who are 'tent-makers'), who are all teachers (as all elders must be 'able to teach', 1 Tim. 3:2): 'The elders who direct the affairs of the church well are worthy of double honour, especially those whose work is preaching and teaching.' Torrance, in *The Eldership in the Reformed Church*, has argued convincingly that Presbyterian elders are much more like deacons in the New Testament (Phil. 1:1; 1 Tim. 3:8–13; cf. 1 Pet. 4:11).

[10] Jobes, *1 Peter*, 296–7.

[11] Achtemeier, *1 Peter*, 326 (Achtemeier's translation).

[12] Michaels, *1 Peter*, 285.

[13] See Bosch, *Transforming Mission*, 222–6, which focuses on the early church's use of various forms of coercion to induce people to embrace the Christian faith. For example, 'Augustine . . . originally regarded coercive measures inadmissible, or at least inappropriate. After 400, however, he gradually came to the conviction that external pressure had a role to play . . . We should, however, keep in mind that Augustine confined coercive measures to fines, confiscation of property, exile and the like' (p. 223).

[14] Bosch, *Transforming*, 223.

[15] See Longenecker and Martin, *Challenging Catholics*, 37–72.

[16] Brown, ed., *New International Dictionary*, II, 511.

[17] Brown, ed., *New International Dictionary*, II, 514–16.

[18] Achtemeier, *1 Peter*, 328.

[19] Achtemeier, *1 Peter*, 329

[20] Cf. Riggans, *Hebrews*, 176: 'Sadly, we are now living in an age when large numbers of believers find it difficult to accept the concept of any spiritual leadership. Many are convinced that our fellowships and congregations are not nearly as strong as they should be because of this lack of proper cohesion and integration under anointed leadership.'

5. Authoritarianism and Feminism

[1] Michaels, *1 Peter*, 277.

[2] Bauckham, *Gospel Women*, 214: 'Prisca or Priscilla is always mentioned in association with her husband Aquila, even though, contrary to normal custom, she is usually placed first in the pair (Acts 18:26; Rom. 16:3; 1 Cor. 16:19; 2 Tim. 4:19), probably because she was more

prominent in Christian antiquity.' Also Torrance, *The Eldership in the Reformed Church*, 12: 'The most well-known of these is the catacomb of Aquila and Priscilla, where the seven presbyters (including Priscilla as a presbytera!) are depicted in a semi-circle behind the Holy Table with Aquila in the centre as their *prestos* or presiding presbyter-bishop, and the deacons in front with the baskets of offerings.'

[3] Bauckham, *Gospel Women*, 269.

[4] Quoted in Bauckham, *Gospel Women*, 270.

[5] Bauckham, *Gospel Women*, 273.

[6] Bauckham, *Gospel Women*, 273.

[7] Bauckham, *Gospel Women*, 271.

[8] Bauckham, *Gospel Women*, 275.

[9] Bauckham, *Gospel Women*, 275. Cf. Mark 10:31, etc.

[10] Bauckham, *Gospel Women*, 280.

[11] Bauckham, *Gospel Women*, 286; cf. France, *Women in the Church's Ministry*, 73–96. France argues that the primary basis of interpretation of Paul's approach to women in church leadership should be Galatians 3:28: 'There is neither Jew nor Gentile, neither slave nor free, neither male nor female, for you are all one in Christ Jesus', rather than the prohibitions of 1 Timothy 2:12: 'I do not permit a woman to teach or to assume authority over a man; she must be quiet.' France cites as support Bruce, *Commentary on Galatians*, 190.

[12] Bauckham, *Gospel Women*, 291.

[13] Bauckham, *Gospel Women*, 293.

[14] Michaels, *1 Peter*, 289.

[15] Michaels, *1 Peter*, 154 (Michaels's translation).

[16] Excessive female personal ornamentation was also condemned in Isaiah 3:18–24 (*c.* 700 BCE), and in a large number of Jewish and Greco–Roman sources with which the New Testament writers would have been familiar.

[17] Achtemeier, *1 Peter*, 212: 'Early Christianity appealed to people of the widest variety of economic situations.' Cf. Michaels, who is more cautious: 'Peter was situated over 1,000 miles away from the churches to which he wrote, and he was in no position to know their economic status, rich or poor' (*1 Peter*, 172).

[18] Michaels, *1 Peter*, 165.

[19] Michaels, *1 Peter*, 166.

[20] Achtemeier, *1 Peter*, 211.

[21] See Trible, *Texts of Terror*.

²² Achtemeier, *1 Peter*, 217.

²³ Achtemeier, *1 Peter*, 218.

²⁴ Achtemeier, *1 Peter*, 219.

²⁵ The texts with which we need to engage are 1 Corinthians 14:33–5 and 1 Timothy 2:11–12. It is helpful to place these alongside each other and to compare their contexts with that of 1 Peter. The latter is culturally more comparable with the Petrine material, as Timothy had been left in charge of the work in the Asian city of Ephesus during the time Paul was awaiting his trial before Caesar in Rome, in the early 60s CE. It is likely that Paul was released, having established his innocence, and then travelled to Crete and other new territories, perhaps including Spain. This is indicated in his letter to Titus, and hinted at in Romans 15:28, which describe his activities and plans before the imperial edicts were issued by Nero following the fire of Rome in 65 CE, which probably led to his subsequent arrest, imprisonment and execution, as alluded to in 2 Timothy. Because of that, we need to interpret Paul's instructions to Timothy in a context which was very similar to that which we have sought to understand in the above discussion. Timothy was overseeing the work in Ephesus, which five years or so earlier had been the responsibility of Priscilla and Aquila. We have noted Luke's account, in Acts, of the important place which Paul accorded, together, to these two key figures. It was not that Priscilla was just the cultural appendage of her husband, and therefore mentioned as if in his shadow. The fact is that she was outstanding in apostolic circles, as a heroine of faith, as far as Luke and Paul are concerned. One might argue, however, that, like the female judge Deborah allegedly was in the Old Testament (Judges 4 – 5), Priscilla was the 'exception that proved the rule' as far as the appointment of leadership among God's people goes. But that interpretation causes far more problems than it may appear to solve, and flies in the face of what we know of Luke's erudition, both as a theologian and as a historian. Luke's purpose, in other words, was counter-cultural, and his choice of material reflects his theological purpose as well as his desire faithfully to report the story of Christian origins in a historically competent way. So it was in the Ephesian church, in which Priscilla was revered as a former overseer, that 1 Timothy 2:11–15 was first read to a congregation. Yet Paul charges his hearers, 'A woman should learn in quietness and full submission. I do not permit a woman to teach or to assume authority over a man; she must be

quiet. For Adam was formed first, then Eve. And Adam was not the one deceived, it was the woman who was deceived and became a sinner. But women will be saved through childbearing – if they continue in faith, love and holiness with propriety.' On the surface, this statement seems to be in direct conflict with Paul's praxis in Acts, because he clearly had permitted – even commissioned – Priscilla so to teach, and Luke commends her for being instrumental, with Aquila, in the instruction of Apollos, who turned out to be a key player in the mission of the early church. Timothy would have known all about that, as would many in the Ephesian house churches. The response to that, by some scholars, is to note that Priscilla is never mentioned alone, but always with her husband, and that she was able to act as an elder/overseer only as she was 'covered', in some theologically and/or culturally appropriate way, by her husband's inherent authority to lead. Others suggest that 1 Timothy 2:12 is not a ban on all women exercising teaching ministry in a congregation, but rather forbids the inappropriate exercise of authority by some married women who did not appreciate the biblical and natural order, and did not acknowledge the proper headship of their husbands. Hence the appeal, they argue, to the authoritative order of Adam over Eve, and to the creation ordinance of marriage, to which Paul had, at least five years earlier, alluded in Ephesians 5:22–33. However, there is another factor which must be accounted for in Paul's message to Timothy here: the fact that it may be advice rather than apostolic command. Paul uses a device here which distinguishes his non–negotiable statements from instruction which is culturally conditioned. In 1 Timothy 2:8–12 he says, 'I want the men everywhere to pray, lifting up holy hands without anger or disputing . . . I also want the women to dress modestly, with decency and propriety . . . I do not permit a woman to teach.' These are his wishes for their contemporary cultural context, in other words, rather than universal principles. It is also clear, from 1 Corinthians 11:5, that women could pray and prophesy in public worship, so that when Paul said '. . . as in all the congregations of the Lord's people. Women should remain silent in the churches. They are not allowed to speak, but must be in submission, as the law says' (1 Corinthians 14:33b–34), he was either referring to regular teaching ministry, or he was forbidding any inappropriate speech, rather than banning any meaningful female contribution to worship (see Houston, *Prophecy Now*, 140–43).

It is probable that his appeal to 'the Law' (Torah) is to be understood in a similar way to his allusion to Genesis 1 and 2 in 1 Timothy 2. Perhaps, then, we can understand Peter's confusion, as expressed in 2 Peter 3:16, where he reflects on Paul's teaching: 'His letters contain some things that are hard to understand, which ignorant and unstable people distort, as they do the other Scriptures, to their own destruction.' Our verdict in this question, therefore, may have to remain open, but that does not mean that we should set up an imagined insurmountable barrier between Peter and Paul, on the interpretation of this issue in particular, or that there is no hope of further scholarly light being shed on the matter. In the meantime, the proposal of this book is that 1 Peter provides a great deal of guidance and understanding for the ongoing debate about the role of women in the leadership of the churches, in the context of Peter's wider concerns about discouraging domineering leadership. See Thiselton, *1 Corinthians*, 250–53; also Marshall, *The Pastoral Epistles*, 436–70.

[26] Brown, ed., *New International Dictionary*, II, 159–63.

[27] Brown, ed., *New International Dictionary*, II, 160.

[28] Brown, ed., *New International Dictionary*, II, 161.

[29] Bruce, *1 and 2 Corinthians*, 103. See also Pierce and Groothuis, *Discovering Biblical Equality*. For the opposing view see Grudem, *Evangelical Feminism and Biblical Truth*.

6. Authorities and Powers

[1] *Naming the Powers: The Language of Power in the New Testament*, 1984; *Unmasking the Powers: The Invisible Forces That Determine Human Existence*, 1986; *Engaging the Powers: Discernment and Resistance in a World of Domination*, 1992 (all Philadelphia: Fortress Press).

[2] See Nielsen, *Solzhenitsyn's Religion*, 84.

[3] For a similar theory of 'apostolic mission circles', Petrine, Pauline, Jacobean and Johannine, see Ellis, *Making*, 45–47, etc.

[4] See Ellis's recent robust defence of the authenticity of 2 Peter in *Making*, 293ff.

[5] Peck, *People*, 123.

[6] See Page, *Powers of Evil*, 230–38, 254–5; Michaels, *1 Peter*, 218–22, 297–304.

[7] See Cullmann, *Christ and Time*, 198. As Page notes: 'During the interim between his resurrection and return, Christ exercises his

lordship over these powers. Though they may seem to act independently of his control, they are not free to do so. To use Cullmann's analogy, they are, as it were, bound to a rope that can be lengthened to give an appearance of freedom. Throughout this period there is ongoing conflict between Christ and the powers, but they repeatedly suffer defeat, and their ultimate doom is assured' (*Powers*, 242).

[8] Page, *Powers*, 244.

[9] Page, *Powers*, 246.

[10] Peretti, *This Present Darkness*. Cf. C.S. Lewis: 'There are two equal and opposite errors into which our race can fall about the devils. One is to disbelieve in their existence. The other is to believe, and to feel an excessive and unhealthy interest in them' (*The Screwtape Letters*, 9).

[11] 'For such persons are false apostles, deceitful workers, masquerading as apostles of Christ. And no wonder, for Satan himself masquerades as an angel of light. It is not surprising, then, if his servants masquerade as servants of righteousness. Their end will be what their actions deserved" (2 Cor. 11:13–15).

[12] Gnosticism developed in the latter half of the first century CE, and involved initiation into mysterious insights (*gnosis*), which might purport to provide knowledge of the tactics and objectives of evil powers.

[13] Wink, *Unmasking*, 4.

[14] Achtemeier, *1 Peter*, 342 (Achtemeier's translation of 1 Pet. 5:9).

[15] 'For our struggle is not against flesh and blood, but against the rulers, against the authorities . . . spiritual forces of evil' (Eph. 6:12); 'The god of this age has blinded the minds of unbelievers, so that they cannot see the light of the gospel that displays the glory of Christ, who is the image of God. For what we preach is not ourselves, but Jesus Christ as Lord, and ourselves as your servants for Jesus' sake' (2 Cor. 4:4–5).

[16] Michaels, *1 Peter*, 300.

[17] Michaels, *1 Peter*, 302.

[18] Achtemeier, *1 Peter*, 344.

[19] Otto Betz in Brown, ed., *New International Dictionary*, II, 606–11.

[20] Brown, ed., *New International Dictionary*, 609.

[21] Brown, ed., *New International Dictionary*, 610; cf. Green, *I believe in Satan's downfall*.

[22] The dynamics of this are described in the Parables of the Kingdom in Matthew 13.

[23] Brown, ed., *New International Dictionary*, 611. See Needham, *2000 Years* (Vol. 3), 96, 107–9.

24 The historian Lord Acton (1834–1902) in a letter to Bishop Creighton, 1887.

25 Wink, *Unmasking*, 4.

26 Peck, *People*, 206.

27 Wink, *Unmasking*, 4.

7. Under God's Hand

1 Hillyer, *1 and 2 Peter, Jude*, 144.

2 Vitz, *Psychology as Religion*, xiv.

3 Vitz, *Psychology*, 21

4 Vitz, *Psychology*, 19. Cf. Mounce, *Matthew*, 39: 'It is the meek who will "inherit the land and enjoy great peace" (Psalm 37:11). "Those of gentle spirit" (NEB), not the grasping and the greedy, receive from life its most satisfying rewards. The aggressive are unable to enjoy their ill-gotten gains. Only the meek have the capacity to enjoy in life all those things that provide genuine and lasting satisfaction.'

5 Vitz, *Psychology*, 26.

6 Vitz, *Psychology*, 31.

7 Moynagh, *Changing World, Changing Church*, 33–4.

8 Vitz, *Psychology*, 33–4.

9 Peck, *People of the Lie*.

10 Tom Wright, *Mark for Everyone*, 140.

11 Wright, *Mark*, 141.

12 Wright, *Mark*, 142.

13 Yet Paul said, in Romans 12:2, 'Do not conform any longer to the pattern of this world, but be transformed by the renewing of your mind.'

14 Ba'al (the name means 'lord') was worshipped as a territorial god by neighbouring nations to Israel, as described in the Ugaritic texts discovered at Ras Shamra, in modern Lebanon. Elijah confronted the prophets of Ba'al at Mount Carmel (1 Kgs. 18:16–40), as King Ahab had adopted their idolatrous religion and many in Israel had followed his lead. Yet God told Elijah that there were 7,000 whose knees had not bowed down to Ba'al (19:18).

15 Vitz, *Psychology*, 42.

16 Vitz, *Psychology*, 76.

17 Vitz, *Psychology*, 77.

18 Vitz, *Psychology*, 84.

[19] Vitz, *Psychology*, 103.

[20] Vitz, *Psychology*, 104.

[21] Vitz, *Psychology*, 130.

[22] Vitz, *Psychology*, 132.

[23] 'A dispute also arose among them as to which of them was considered to be greatest. Jesus said to them "The kings of the Gentiles lord it over them . . . But you are not to be like that . . . I am among you as one who serves."'

[24] Christopher Wright, *Deuteronomy*, 210.

[25] Wright, *Deuteronomy*, 27.

[26] Wright, *Deuteronomy*, 215.

[27] Vitz, *Psychology*, 160.

[28] Vitz, *Psychology*, 160.

[29] Vitz, *Psychology*, 162.

[30] Burns, *The Feeling Good Handbook*, 394.

8. Mending Networks

[1] You is plural here in Greek.

[2] Achtemeier, *1 Peter*, 346.

[3] Hillyer, *1 and 2 Peter*, 149.

[4] Hillyer, *1 and 2 Peter*, 146.

[5] Hillyer, *1 and 2 Peter*, 146.

[6] 'Believers can safely leave all anxieties with their heavenly Father (Matt. 6:25–34). He will care about their cares. For their part, believers are to be care-free. It is one of the distinctive treasures which Christianity has inherited from Judaism that God is known to be concerned with the personal care of his people. Other religions at best see God as aloof, as one who, while good and perfect, keeps his distance from human beings.' (Hillyer, *1 and 2 Peter*, 145).

[7] Achtemeier, *1 Peter*, 117 (Achtemeier's translation).

[8] Michaels, *1 Peter*, 54.

[9] Achtemeier, *1 Peter*, 117.

[10] 'Love the LORD your God with all your heart and with all your soul and with all your strength.'

[11] G. Harder in Brown, ed., *New International Dictionary*, III, 127.

[12] Burns, 'The Ten Forms of Twisted Thinking' in *Feeling Good*, 8–11.

[13] Passantino, 'Psychology and the Church'.

[14] Williams, et al., *I'm Not Supposed to Feel Like This*.

15 Williams, et al., *I'm Not*, 127–49.

16 Williams, et al., *I'm Not*, 175.

17 Williams, et al., *I'm Not*, 10.

18 Burns, *Feeling Good*, xiv–xxviii.

19 Burns, *Feeling Good*, xix.

20 Burns, *Feeling Good*, xxix.

21 Craig, *The Scots' Crisis of Confidence*, 290–91.

22 Warren, *The Purpose Driven Church*.

23 In Collins, ed., *2000 years of Classic Christian Prayers*, 296.

24 'We hold these truths to be self–evident, that all men are created equal, that they are endowed by their Creator with certain inalienable rights, that among these are Life, Liberty, and the pursuit of Happiness.' Of course, 'all men' did not include slaves or native Americans!

25 Lingenfelter and Mayers, *Ministering*, 18.

26 Lingenfelter and Mayers, *Ministering*, 24.

27 Lingenfelter and Mayers, *Ministering*, 27–8.

9. Leading Habits and Purpose

1 See the website of The Watchman Fellowship, www.watchman.org. for a full treatment of Covey's management theories and Mormon theology.

2 Covey, *Divine Center*, 240.

3 Covey, *Divine Center*, 34–5.

4 This information came from the website of Christ Church, Virginia Water, Surrey, England. www.cc-vw.org, originally accessed July 2006.

5 *The Times*, London, 14 January 2006.

6 See Brown, ed., *New International Dictionary*, II, 437–8.

7 See Marshall, *Acts*, 39–42.

8 'Despite our claims that our organizations and churches are families, most of them are run like corporations' (Fernando, *Jesus Driven*, 26).

9 2 Peter 1:5–9 addresses the issue of effectiveness, and the need for Christians to develop qualities such as faith, goodness, knowledge, self-control, perseverance, godliness, brotherly kindness and love. Peter adds, 'For if you possess these qualities in increasing measure,

they will keep you from being *ineffective* and unproductive in your knowledge of our Lord Jesus Christ' (2 Pet. 1:8).

10 D. Muller, in Brown, ed., *New International Dictionary*, III, 1016.

11 'Israel went after other gods because they thought they could provide the desired blessings of rain, fertility, success, victory, etc. The tragic irony is that the pursuit of such idolatries ultimately brought the dire opposite of what those false gods promised. There is a persistent tendency in human society towards idolatry – seeking answers and solutions in everything but the living God. Modern western idolatries include the ideologies of materialism ("the Market"), consumerism, individualism, militarism, etc., but these do not give the salvation they appear to promise' (Wright, *Deuteronomy*, 282, commenting on Deut. 28).

12 'Often, indeed, the true purpose of a process only appears at the end. The end reveals the purpose' (Mitton, *The Epistle of James*, 190).

13 Covey, *Living*, 126.

14 Aikman, *Jesus in Beijing*.

15 Covey, *Living*, frontispiece.

16 Covey, *Living*, frontispiece.

17 Covey, *Living*, frontispiece.

10. Leading Examples Look East – Peter's Paradigm

1 Classical Greek *paradeigma*, 'proof, example, model'; in the New Testament, with the same meaning, *hypodeigma*: John 13:15; Hebrews 4:11; James 5:10; 2 Peter 2:6.

2 Ellis, *Making*, 366.

3 Bosch, *Transforming*, 181–9.

4 For a classical treatment, see Allen, *Missionary Methods – St Paul's or Ours?*

5 'Leaders are people who do the right things; managers are people who do things right. Both roles are crucial, but they differ profoundly' (Bennis, *Why Leaders Can't Lead*, 18).

6 Analytic thinking takes things apart; synthetic thinking brings things together.

7 See Bonhoeffer, *Letters and Papers from Prison*, 8.

8 Narramore, *No Condemnation: Rethinking Guilt Motivation in Counselling, Preaching, and Parenting*.

9 Narramore, *No Condemnation*, 310–11.

[10] Fung, *The Isaiah Vision*, 43–4.

[11] Philip Yancey, *Prayer*, 97. For a critique of the influence of modernism in the Western church, using the fast-food metaphor, see Drane, *The McDonaldization of the Church*. Despite the title, Drane does not address the issue of branding, but he makes this telling comment: 'The "purpose-driven church" . . . is clearly the sort of atmosphere in which upwardly mobile corporate achievers would feel at home, because much of the thinking behind it came from the world of business in the first place (p. 81). See also Webster, *Selling Jesus*.

[12] Fung, *Isaiah Vision*, 44.

[13] Fung, *Isaiah Vision*, 45–6.

[14] Fung, *Isaiah Vision*, 46.

[15] Fung, *Isaiah Vision*, 46

[16] Fung, *Isaiah Vision*, 47.

[17] Newbigin, *The Gospel*, 222–33.

[18] 'For what we preach is not ourselves but Jesus Christ as Lord and ourselves as your servants for Jesus' sake' (2 Cor. 4:5).

[19] Jeal, *Livingstone*, 1.

[20] Maxwell, *Your Attitude: Key to Success*, 79–80.

[21] 'If emerging church leaders wish to become a long-term prophetic voice . . . they must listen carefully to criticisms of their movement as they transparently want others to listen to them. They need to spend more time in careful study of Scripture and theology than they are doing . . . They need to take great pains not to distort history and theology alike, by not caricaturing their opponents and not playing manipulative games' (Carson, *Becoming Conversant*, 234).

[22] Aikman, *Jesus in Beijing*, 290–91. Wang Mingdao (1900–91) was one of China's leading Christian 'patriarchs' during the years of communist persecution. As Aikman notes, 'Without the political implications, he was the Nelson Mandela of Chinese Christianity' (*Jesus in Beijing*, 47).

BIBLIOGRAPHY

Achtemeier, Paul J. *1 Peter*. Hermeneia Series. Minneapolis: Augsburg Fortress, 1996.

Adair, John A. *The Leadership of Jesus*. Norwich: Canterbury Press, 2001.

Aikman, David. *Jesus in Beijing*. London: Monarch, 2005.

Allen, Roland. *Missionary Methods – St Paul's or Ours?* Grand Rapids: Eerdmans, 1962, first published 1912.

Bauckham, Richard. *Gospel Women: Studies of the named women in the Gospels*. Grand Rapids: Eerdmans, 2002.

Bennett, David W. *Leadership Images from the New Testament*. Carlisle: OM Publishing, 1998.

Bennis, Warren. *Why Leaders Can't Lead: The Unconscious Conspiracy Continues*. San Francisco: Jossey-Bass, 1989.

Bonhoeffer Dietrich. *Letters and Papers from Prison*. London: Fontana, 1959.

Bosch, David J. *Transforming Mission: Paradigm Shifts in the Theology of Mission*. Maryknoll, NY: Orbis, 1991.

Brown, Colin, ed. *New International Dictionary of New Testament Theology*, 3 Vols. Grand Rapids: Zondervan, 1975, 1976, 1978.

Bruce, F.F. *Commentary on Galatians*. Exeter: Paternoster Press, 1982.

—. *1 and 2 Corinthians* (New Century Bible). London: Oliphants, 1971.

Burns, David D. *The Feeling Good Handbook*. 2nd ed. New York: Penguin Putnam, 1999.

Card, Michael A. *A Fragile Stone: the Emotional Life of Simon Peter*. Downers Grove: Inter-Varsity Press, 2003.

Carson, D.A. *Becoming Conversant with the Emerging Church*. Grand Rapids: Zondervan, 2005

Catechism of the Catholic Church. 2nd ed. English Translation. London: Geoffrey Chapman, 1997.

Chester, Andrew and Ralph P. Martin. *The Theology of the Letters of James, Peter and Jude.* Cambridge: Cambridge Univ. Press, 1994.

Collins, Owen, ed. *2000 years of Classic Christian Prayers.* Maryknoll: Orbis, 1999.

Covey, Stephen R. *The Divine Center.* Salt Lake City: Bookcraft Publications, 1982.

—. *The 7 Habits of Highly Effective People.* New York: Simon and Schuster, 1989.

—. *Living the 7 Habits.* New York: Simon and Schuster, 1999.

Craig, Carol. *The Scots' Crisis of Confidence.* Edinburgh: Big Thinking, 2003.

Cullmann, Oscar. *Christ and Time.* London: SCM Press, 1951.

Drane, John. *The McDonaldization of the Church.* London: Darton, Longman and Todd, 2000.

Elliott, John H. *A Home for the Homeless: a Sociological Exegesis of 1 Peter, its Situation and Strategy.* London: SCM Press, 1982

Ellis, E. Earle. *The Making of the New Testament Documents.* Boston and Leiden: Brill, 2002.

Fernando, Ajith. *Jesus Driven Ministry.* Leicester: Inter-Varsity Press, 2003.

France, R.T. *Women in the Church's Ministry.* Carlisle: Paternoster Press, 1995.

Fung, Raymond. *The Isaiah Vision.* Geneva: World Council of Churches, 1992.

Giuliani, Rudolph W. *Leadership.* New York: Miramax, 2002.

Green, Michael. *I believe in Satan's downfall.* London: Hodder and Stoughton, 1981.

Griffiths, Michael. *The Example of Jesus.* London: Hodder and Stoughton, 1985.

Grudem, Wayne. *Evangelical Feminism and Biblical Truth.* Leicester: Inter-Varsity Press, 2005.

Haggai, John E. *The Seven Secrets of Effective Business Relationships.* London: HarperCollins, 1999.

Harding, Mark. *Early Christian Life and Thought in Social Context.* London and New York: T&T Clark, 2003.

Hill, Alexander. *Just Business: Christian Ethics for the Market Place.* Carlisle: Paternoster Press, 1998.

Hillyer, Norman. *1 and 2 Peter, Jude.* New International Biblical Commentary. Carlisle: Paternoster Press, 1992.

Houston, Graham. *Prophecy Now.* Leicester: Inter-Varsity Press, 1989.

—. *Virtual Morality: Christian Ethics in the Computer Age.* Leicester: Apollos, 1998.

Hurtado, Larry W. *Mark.* New International Biblical Commentary. Carlisle: Paternoster Press, 1989.

Jeal, Tim. *Livingstone.* New Haven and London: Yale University Press, 2001.

Jobes, Karen H. *1 Peter.* Baker Exegetical Commentary on the New Testament. Grand Rapids: Baker, 2005.

Kelly, J.N.D. *Commentary on the Epistles of Peter and Jude.* London: A&C Black, 1969.

Kittel, G., ed. *Theological Dictionary of the New Testament.* Grand Rapids: Eerdmans, 1974.

Lewis, C.S. *The Screwtape Letters.* London: Geoffrey Bles, 1942.

Lingenfelter, Sherwood G. and Marvin K. Mayers. *Ministering Cross-Culturally.* Grand Rapids: Baker, 1986.

Longenecker, Dwight and John Martin. *Challenging Catholics.* Carlisle: Paternoster Press, 2001.

Marshall, I. Howard. *1 Peter.* Downers Grove and Leicester: Inter-Varsity Press, 1991.

—. *The Acts of the Apostles.* Leicester: Inter-Varsity Press, 1980.

—. *The Epistles of John.* New International Commentary on the NT. Grand Rapids: Eerdmans, 1978.

—. *The Pastoral Epistles.* International Critical Commentary. London: T&T Clark, 1999.

Maxwell, John. *Your Attitude: Key to Success.* San Bernardino, CA: Here's Life Publishers, 1984.

Meeks, Wayne A. *The First Urban Christians: the Social World of the Apostle Paul.* New Haven and London: Yale University Press, 1983.

Michaels, J. Ramsey. *1 Peter.* Word Biblical Commentary. Waco: Word, 1988.

Mitton, C. Leslie. *The Epistle of James.* London: Marshall, Morgan and Scott, 1966.

Mounce, Robert. *Matthew.* New International Biblical Commentary. Carlisle: Paternoster Press, 1995.

Moynagh, Michael. *Changing World, Changing Church*. London: Monarch, 2001.

Narramore, S. Bruce. *No Condemnation: Rethinking Guilt Motivation in Counselling, Preaching, and Parenting*. Eugene, Oregon: Wipf and Stock, 1984.

Needham, N.R. *2000 years of Christ's Power*. 3 Vols. London: Grace Publications, 1998, 2000, 2004.

Newbigin, Lesslie. *The Gospel in a Pluralist Society*. London: SPCK, 1989.

Nielsen, N.C. *Solzhenitsyn's Religion*. London: Mowbrays, 1976.

Page, Sydney H.T. *Powers of Evil: a Biblical Study of Satan and Demons*. Grand Rapids: Baker and Leicester: Apollos, 1995.

Passantino, B. and G. 'Psychology and the Church (Part Three): Can psychotherapy be integrated with Christianity?' Charlotte, North Carolina: Christian Research Institute, 2007.

Peck, M. Scott. *People of the Lie: the Hope for Healing Human Evil*. New York: Simon and Schuster, 1983.

Peretti, Frank. *This Present Darkness*. Wheaton, Illinois: Crossway, 1986 .

Pierce, R.W. and R.M. Groothuis. *Discovering Biblical Equality: Complementarity without Hierarchy*. Downers Grove and Leicester: Inter-Varsity Press, 2004.

Pippert, Rebecca M. *Hope Has Its Reasons*. San Francisco: Harper & Row, 1989.

Riggans, Walter. *Hebrews*. Fearn: Christian Focus, 1998.

Robinson, Martin. *A World Apart: Creating a Church for the Unchurched*. Speldhurst: Monarch, 1992.

Stedman, Ray. *Body Life*. Ventura: Regal Books, 1972.

Thiede, Carsten P. *Simon Peter: from Galilee to Rome*. Exeter: Paternoster Press, 1986.

—. *The Cosmopolitan World of Jesus*. London: SPCK, 2004.

Thiselton, Anthony C. *1 Corinthians: A Shorter Exegetical and Pastoral Commentary*. Grand Rapids: Eerdmans, 2006.

Thurén, Lauri. *Argument and Theology in 1 Peter*. Sheffield: Sheffield Academic Press, 1995.

Torrance, Thomas F. *The Eldership in the Reformed Church*. Edinburgh: Handsel Press, 1984.

Trible, Phyllis. *Texts of Terror: Literary-Feminist Readings of Biblical Narratives*. Philadelphia: Fortress Press, 1984.

Vitz, Paul C. *Psychology as Religion: the Cult of Self Worship*. 2nd ed. Grand Rapids: Eerdmans, 1994.

Walker, Andrew. *Restoring the Kingdom*. London: Hodder and Stoughton, 1985.

Warren, Rick. *The Purpose Driven Church*. Grand Rapids: Zondervan, 1995.

—. *The Purpose Driven Life*. Grand Rapids: Zondervan, 2002.

Watson, David. *I believe in the Church*. London: Hodder and Stoughton, 1978.

Webster, Douglas D. *Selling Jesus: What's Wrong with Marketing the Church*. Downers Grove: Inter-Varsity Press, 1992.

Williams, Chris, et al. *I'm not supposed to feel like this: a Christian self-help approach to depression and anxiety*. London: Hodder and Stoughton, 2002.

Wimber, John. *Power Evangelism*. London: Hodder and Stoughton, 1985.

Wink, Walter. *Unmasking the Powers: The Invisible Forces That Determine Human Existence*. Philadelphia: Fortress Press, 1986.

Wright, Christopher. *Deuteronomy*. New International Biblical Commentary. Carlisle: Paternoster Press, 1996.

Wright, Tom. *Mark for Everyone*. London: SPCK, 2001.

Yancey, Philip. *Prayer: Does it make any difference?* London: Hodder, 2006.

Index

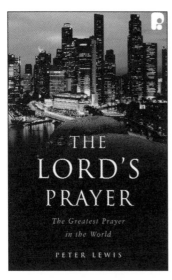

The Lord's Prayer

The Greatest Prayer in the World

Peter Lewis

'Our Father . . .' Quoted, memorised, spoken and sung, the Lord's Prayer is an inspiration to millions. Down the centuries and around the world it has expressed the deepest longings of all true Christians. However, the prayer that Jesus taught his followers reveals something far greater – the character and purposes of God himself. In this sensitive and often moving book, Peter Lewis shows how an intimate relationship with God is a reality that can be experienced today.

'When Peter Lewis comes out with a book, the church is always enriched.' – **R.T. Kendall**

'Peter Lewis is one of the most worshipful pastors I know. His wisdom, humanity and sheer adoration of the greatness of God shine though in this inspirational new edition of *The Lord's Prayer*. It isn't simply an inspiring guide to prayer but also a masterful, tender and powerful entry-level guide to the whole of the Christian life.' – **Julian Hardyman,** Senior Pastor, Eden Baptist Church, Cambridge, England

Peter Lewis leads The Cornerstone Church in Nottingham, England. He has an international speaking ministry and has authored several books.

978-1-84227-601-3

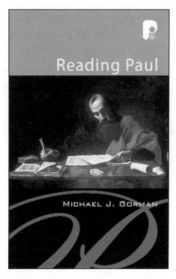

Reading Paul

Michael J. Gorman

In this introduction to Paul and his gospel (written especially for lay readers, beginning students, and those unsure about what to make of the apostle) Gorman takes Paul seriously, as someone who speaks for God and to us. Reading Paul explores the central themes of the apostle's gospel. Gorman places special emphasis on the theo-political character of Paul's gospel and on its themes of cross and resurrection, multiculturalism in the church, peacemaking and non-violence as the way of Christ. Gorman also offers a distinctive interpretation of justification by faith as participation in Christ. Unlike many introductions to Paul, this one makes a contribution to the ongoing discussion of the significance of the apostle, both as an historical figure and as a contemporary voice.

> 'This splendid introduction to the Apostle Paul is the best book of its kind: concise, wise, insightful, thoroughly conversant with the best recent scholarship, yet thoroughly clear and readable.' – **Richard B. Hays**, George Washington Ivey Professor of New Testament, The Divinity School, Duke University, USA

Michael J. Gorman is Professor of Sacred Scripture and Dean of the Ecumenical Institute of Theology at St. Mary's Seminary & University in Baltimore, USA.

978-1-84227-603-7

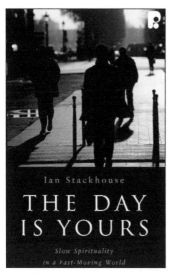

The Day is Yours

Slow Spirituality in a Fast-Moving World

Ian Stackhouse

The Day is Yours is a protest against the culture of speed both in the culture at large, but also, more ominously, in the church itself. Rooted in the monastic liturgy of the hours, *The Day is Yours* argues that in order for Christians to act as a truly prophetic witness, in a time of cultural decadence, they must recover a more biblical rhythm in which work, rest, relationships, worship and prayer are held together in creative tension. Written by a pastor, the central thrust of *The Day is Yours* is that living one day at a time with gratitude and contentedness is vital, lest the church capitulates to the distractedness of modern life.

'Ian Stackhouse has given us a very powerful and persuasive call to embrace a slower, fuller and more biblical rhythm of life. I read it on a day I was forced to take off because of overwork and exhaustion. It helped me to reorder my life so as to live by priorities not pressures. I warmly recommend it!' – **Mark Stibbe**, Vicar of St Andrew's Church, Chorleywood

'Rhythms of life, of worship, of prayer, can be dismissed as onerous by the indolent and the foolish but to the truly wise they provide the heartbeat to spiritual vitality and fruitfulness.' – **John Colwell**, Tutor in Christian Doctrine and Ethics, Spurgeon's College, London

Ian Stackhouse is the Pastoral Leader of the Millmead Centre, home of Guildford Baptist Church, UK. He is author of *The Gospel-Driven Church*.

978-1-84227-600-6

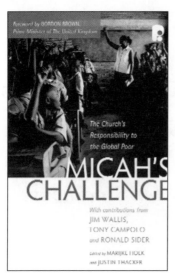

Micah's Challenge

The Church's Responsibility to the Global Poor

Edited by Marijke Hock and Justin Thacker

'He has showed you, O man, what is good. And what does the LORD require of you? To act justly and to love mercy and to walk humbly with your God' (Micah 6:8).

This is Micah's challenge to Israel in his day and to the Church in our day. God called them and us to act with justice, mercy and humility in our dealings with the poor. This book pulls together prophetic voices from Jim Wallis to Tony Campolo and from Ronald Sider to René Padilla and Joel Edwards to explore the theological, ethical and practical dimensions of Micah's challenge. The heart of the book is an exploration of 'acting justly', 'walking humbly', and 'loving mercy'. That call is set within a broader biblical and theological framework and followed by reflections on how we might live it out today. *Micah's Challenge* offers a passionate, biblical, and challenging call to think afresh and to act redemptively as individuals and as Christian communities.

'I warmly welcome this book.' – **Gordon Brown**, Prime Minister of Great Britain

'*Micah's Challenge* – biblical, accessible, uncomfortable and compelling.' – **Steve Chalke** MBE, Founder of Oasis Global and Faithworks

Marikje Hoek works for Network, part of the Evangelical Alliance, and is a visiting lecturer at Regents Theological College, Nantwich; **Justin Thacker** is Head of Theology at the Evangelical Alliance.

978-1-84227-606-8

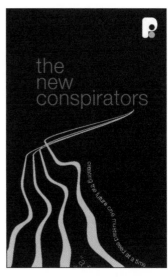

The New Conspirators

Creating the Future One Mustard seed at a Time

Tom Sine

God is doing something fresh through a new generation of 'conspirators'. This new work can be seen in at least four different streams: the emerging, the missional, the mosaic (multicultural church plants) and the monastic. In this book Tom Sine present some of the innovative new models that are being created by those ministering within these diverse streams. He also explores the important questions they are raising for all of us regarding what it means to be a disciple, be the church and do the mission of the church. The book then investigates new challenges facing both our larger global society and the church as we journey together into an increasingly uncertain future. It is a call for all of us to join these new conspirators in discovering creative ways in which God might use our mustard seeds to be a part of what he is doing to manifest his kingdom in the world.

A fabulous book! A bold challenge to all who think the kingdom of God can be built from the starting point of compromise and comfort.' – **Jonny Baker**, Mission leadership and communities team leader with the Church Mission Society

'A great book from a great teacher and genuinely wise guide.' – **Alan Hirsch**, founding director of Forge Mission Training Network

Tom Sine is an author and a Christian speaker with an international ministry. He is founder of Mustard Seed Associates, Seattle, USA.

978-1-84227-559-7